DIFFERENT DRUMMERS

ARE...

BRYN WEAVER

MOVING ALONG!
THE TIME IS NOW...

atmosphere press

CONTENTS

SEASON FOUR: NORTHWARD BOUND

SEASON FIVE: MY UTURN BACK TO THE MIDWEST

SEASON SIX: RETIREMENT AND SCHOOL

SEASON SEVEN: NEW PATH

SEASON EIGHT: DESSERT AND ALL THOSE EXTRAS

CLOSING BELL

OPENING BELL

TO: MY READERS

WELCOME!!

For the most part, I wrote this as though I was talking directly to you, so feel free to join the discussion.

So, your first question might be "WHO DOES SHE THINK SHE IS?" I mean writing a book about her life. Give me a break. There are no brilliant intellectuals, or captivating talent, or extraordinary accomplishments, or a Nobel Prize, so, what's the deal?

I'll tell you what it is. I have a message and direction for life and I'm sharing it with you because I think it's important and valuable. It goes like this.

It is a story of a not-so-good and very difficult beginning and growth and proof that those problems and difficulties i.e., an alcoholic home and loss of love in familial relationships, should not spoil or determine the rest of life's journey. Also, occasional health issues that are manageable should provide, with the assistance of wonderful and supportive friends, resilience and determination but not stop the train. This is important.

With the above in mind, this adventure started because I love to write and I had a story and life's path to share. To add to that, whenever the topic—good, bad or indifferent—came up that was interesting or thoughtful or fun, I would sit down at the typewriter (yes, a typewriter) and tap away. As I got into high school, the subjects were usually assigned but coupled with frequent chaos at home.

Does one carry this home life beginning for their entire

life? It's always there because you experienced it but it need not negatively or sadly mess with your full journey. Hence, my writings about many subjects that are encouraging and fun. Should you seek counsel and guidance along the way? Yes, but remember that life moves forward.

Very simply then, this journey is all about CHOICES—from your heart, head, soul and life experiences. The constant throughout is being able to view life not only with a thoughtful and/or serious consideration but with humor.

Each Season's life story and accompanying writings point in new and/or different directions. Am I going to tell you which directions? NO! It's not my job, your journey is all about your CHOICES.

The SEASONS provide a life story connected to and influenced by geographic locations and culture and great people. Let me tell you now, it has been an amazing journey.

As to the writing, let me be very clear, that old fashioned typewriter was with me for only a very short period of time. Then the big improvement, a computer and word perfect. Talk about an incredible writing tool—I could not only write but could change, correct, add or delete ideas and then make copies. When in college, I started asking a few friends to review and comment on my written word assignments and they are the people who pushed me toward the idea of a book. I'm glad they did—this has been fun.

Read on and thank you for being here.
Bryn W.

SEASON ONE

LIFE'S DOOR IS OPEN

A TIME TO BE

HAPPY,

FUN,

AND

GOOFY

I have arrived.

THE BEGINNING

I HAVE ARRIVED!!

I am a cell and I'm growing in a dark warm place where I am comfortable. As this growth continues, my combination of Irish and German predispositions are attaching themselves to my soul and mind and forming my humanity that in this first stage is devoid of light, speech, experience and behavior. This will change since the good and not-so-good foundations have not yet made an appearance.

This is an upward journey as I move into a world of light and sound and language and all those people. It is a time of childish self-absorption and observation and fun with early definitions of morality and duty. As I moved through the one to five numbers, I recognized a big difference between boy persons and girl persons.

Experience and culture have arrived to begin the process of shaping the baby girl into a girl child. With that growth, there came early awareness that there was a void between some of the incoming language and resulting actions. With no depth of thought, I recognized that something was not quite right.

No writings at this time. I haven't located my alphabet.

Moving upward...

CLOSE CALL
- THE FIRST

At the age of five, I was in the hospital having my tonsils removed. An ether tank exploded in the operating room and set the room on fire.

An orderly in an adjacent room put a wet sheet on himself and pulled me from the room.

I had frizzled hair but that was all.

THOUGHT FOR THE DAY:
KNOW THAT EVERY DAY IS A GIFT.

SEASON TWO

GREAT GROWTH

IN KNOWLEDGE, HEIGHT, WEIGHT,

KNOW-IT-ALL ATTITUDE AND

VERY EXCITING.

It is all about me.

IT IS ALL ABOUT ME.

This time period had four areas of time that were defined by my age and the environment around me. My involvement in these time periods ran the gamut from no decision making in the first and being completely in charge of my life during number four. It was very exciting.

First, my grade school experience was parochial and strong on academics and religion. Except for some ongoing distractions at home, this was an excellent time. For clarity, these distractions were more apparent when returning to an alcoholic home after school until I was out of High School. My Father had been an alcoholic most of his life and it carried forward while his children were in school.

Second, I entered high school at 12 and thoroughly enjoyed every minute of my four year experience. Not unlike grade school, it was strong on academics and religion but, perhaps of more importance, we were instilled with a strong grounding of ethics, integrity and values. Since college was not on my horizon for many years, I have always been grateful for that academic and value-based education. My only problems were after school, as noted above, and that distraction and/or chaos continued through my High School years.

Third, I entered the world of work at age 16 and that became another time of amazing growth as I moved from peer contact to adult contact. I approached going to college but was told that my role was to work at a nice little office job, get married, have children and stay home, and I didn't need a college education to accomplish these tasks. Although I had no specific objection to that path, I thought I should make my own life's choices and at that time, I was simply not mature enough to know how to deal with that family directive. The home problems that were recognized before ten and experienced in my teens unfortunately continued after High School even absent the alcohol, and were reaching into all areas of my life and promoted my early maturation. I was 17, 18 19 and 20 going on 40.

So, what did I do between 16 and 20? The driving force during this time was my Mother who was a good person but very old fashioned and dedicated and open to ideas only for my male siblings. She was determined that I get a "nice little office job", marriage, etc. as I've already said, so, with that in mind, what would be my first adventure? Business school, of course, where I could learn to be a good secretary. It consisted of more lessons on typing, learning shorthand, how to write letters, answering phones in offices, etc., etc. The school sent me to Nelly Don, a local women's clothing business, for my first temporary job. I actually enjoyed it for a while since, for the first time in my life, I was making my own money. That was fun.

There were many jobs during this time and three things were very apparent. First, I was good at being a secretary; second, because this was one of the predominant fields for women, I would always have a job; and finally, I was one very bored teenager. Since there weren't many other careers for women in those days, I started looking at other options. This became an adventure in itself since one of the choices was to move away from my family and Midwestern cultural environment. I needed to be living in an environment free of chaos and where I could grow as a human being and determine my own path. I did much research on this move looking at where in the country I would fit and then, before I made my decision, I got lucky.

Along came a coworker and her husband, Carola and Hubert (both immigrants from Germany), who were going to move to San Francisco and told me if I ever decided to leave the Midwest and move west, I could stay with them until I got settled. Talk about an open door! I owe much to these two and we remained close friends for many years. I thanked them frequently for their generosity and was finally able to say thank you in an appropriate way when I sponsored Hubert when he became a U.S. Citizen.

Now add to that, I was working for an insurance company and my current Boss called the San Francisco office of this company to see if they needed some secretarial help. They did, so I had a job when I got there. Everything fell in place—this was a move that was destined to happen, thank goodness for me.

Finally, at the age of 20 (or 40 depending on how one views maturity), I moved to San Francisco. Frankly, it saved me—I was now allowed to grow and be the person I wanted to be and, perhaps more important, achieve and enjoy this experience in a calm and happy environment that was such an improvement over my family home life.

Before I change geography, take a look at the writings noted in SEASON TWO. They are especially important to this period of my life. Now get ready to travel West.

TO: MY READERS
RE: **THOUGHTS AND GUIDANCE FOR THE JOURNEY**
DATE: LIFETIME

1. Every day is a gift. The quality of your life is the gift you give to yourself. It is all up to you.

2. Never miss a chance to keep your mouth shut.

3. Peace is not exclusively the absence of war. It is a virtue, a state of mind, a disposition for benevolence and justice.

4. When you are wrong, be willing to change; when you are right, be easy to live with.

5. Act and think only on those things that can bear the full light of day and travel the path of integrity without looking back, for there is never a wrong time to do the right thing.

6. The bad news is time flies. The good news is you're the pilot.

7. Never be bullied into silence.

8. A balanced diet is a chocolate chip cookie in each hand.

9. Accept no one's definition of your life. Define yourself.

10. **AND NEVER FORGET:** That while life is tough, there are always Life Savers, Fritos and Macaroni and Cheese.

THE DRUM BEAT
OF MY EXISTENCE

I can hear my heart beat. I started hearing it years ago. I'm not sure why I hear it nor are the physicians in my life but this drum beat of my existence continues.

Is it a reminder of the fragility of my life? Of all life? Maybe it keeps me from taking things for granted. Whatever the reason, it gives me pause to think about my past, the person I've become and ponder if there are some things I should be doing, or as my Grandmother might say "your work isn't done yet.

In looking back, I realize how my heart beat progressed. From age 14 to about 40 or thereabouts, we are all immortal. We take risks, act foolishly and occasionally wisely, but mostly we just live our lives to the fullest. We pursue an education and/or career, fall in love, suffer a lost love, get married, have children, stay single, travel, and buy all the "stuff" we need and most of the "stuff" we just want. Maybe we have spiritual or conscience driven priorities or possibly no priorities at all. No matter the path we choose, out sense of immortality remains.

Somewhere in our 40s (give or take), we become aware of our mortality. It's very unsettling. Our immortality is gone and we come face to face with the thought that none of us are getting out of this life alive. As nearly as I can figure, this mortality light bulb is more likely to flash on in our hearts and minds when we lose someone. Whoever this person is, they are up close and personal and leave us before we think they should. Or we can face our mortality when we experience one of life's "close calls." In my case, it was being on a commercial flight that had only one engine and one landing gear as we prepared for a crash landing. Whatever or whoever it is, we're never quite the same again.

Once we get past the grief and/or anxiety, we have a great opportunity. Actually, being aware of your mortality can free you up to start looking at or fully participating in all those daily and personal choices or directions or plans that you've thought about.

So, now turn the page and remember, this is all about you and me.

<u>CONSIDER THE FOLLOWING:</u>

1. HAVE AT LEAST ONE GOOD LAUGH A DAY.

2. TAKE YOUR WORK SERIOUSLY — NOT YOURSELF.

3. EXERCISE YOUR MIND AND BODY.

4. BE THOUGHTFUL AND KIND.

5. HOLD YOURSELF ACCOUNTABLE.

6. HELP OTHERS. YOU WILL ALWAYS GET MORE OUT OF THIS THAN YOU GIVE.

7. INDULGE IN COMMON SENSE.

8. GIVE YOURSELF A BREAK!

WHAT A WOMAN

Since the problems in my home were sometimes a little difficult and as I moved into my teenage years, they moved from "a little" to "a lot", I found myself stressed and needing to "step away" in order to recoup who I was and calm down and initiate some emotional recovery. It was only a little step—-to my neighbors.

Our back doors were twenty-five feet apart. Down four steps, walk the footage, up four steps and I arrived. Very easy, incredibly important. The neighbors consisted of a Mom (Marsha), Dad and a daughter who was my age and it was this Mom's presence that allowed me to periodically rescue myself by doing the down/walk/up dance.

So, when issues, language, attitudes, etc. got too difficult and where I was the recipient of too much attention, I would head for the back door, do the twenty-five feet, knock on the door, and have a wonderful and rescuing greeting along the lines of "Bryn, how nice to see you. Come in. Want some milk (or tea) and cookies?" We sat at the small breakfast nook table, and while she continued to read her book, I indulged in the milk and cookies and enjoyed some recovery. This time was quiet and emotionally settling in the presence of a woman who knew the importance of this down time for me and quietly displayed the much needed care and love. How fortunate I was.

Pushing forward many years, after 38 years on the West Coast and returning to the Midwest, I was again pleased and happy to be in this same wonderful woman's presence again. Still that same gracious, warm, kind demeanor that repeated,

"Bryn, how nice to see you."

One Sunday evening in 1995, I remember a particular visit. Unfortunately, she had been given a somewhat shortened medical prognosis, so while she was still up and walking around, her time was limited. I stood in her living room looking out the window at the flowers in the yard. She moved closer, put her arm around my waist and I put my arm around her shoulder. We held like that for a while and she told me about the flowers and how they would grow and then she said "I hope I'm here to see them." One side of my heart was deeply saddened but the other side was filled with gratitude for my time with her and how important she was in my life.

We lost Marsha a few months later and again I experienced the emotional duality of sorrow associated with great gratitude. As I have reflected on my time with her and especially our shared moment in time on that Sunday evening looking at the flowers, I frequently think of the song WIND BENEATH MY WINGS and the question from that song that resonates from me to her even now.

I ask: "Did you ever know that you're my hero?"

Thank you, dear Marsha.

Thank Heavens for..............

MY DECISION MAKER

This connection starts with one of those family to family events. Mary and her brothers were part of that family and I got to connect with all three. See the "Siblings" information in the in SEASON FIVE section of the journey.

I met Mary when she was visiting her family in the Midwest and before I moved to the West Coast. At that time I was 19 and living at home with my parents and she was 29, married, with one child and living on the east coast. Somehow and with great good fortune we wound up sitting next to each other at an outdoor musical. In the course of our conversations, she invited me to visit her and her family and spend a week getting to know D.C. I was thrilled and accepted the invitation.

As a side note, this would be my first traveling by myself, an event that caused some mild trepidation at home. In addition to D.C., I visited cousins in Philadelphia and my friend Carol in New Jersey. What an exciting time for a 19 year old.

Back to Mary. After I arrived in D.C., we did some sightseeing together and she turned me loose to do my own thing. It was nice to be treated like a grownup. One afternoon, when I wasn't out and about, Mary and I discussed the similarities in our families and shared culture. I shared with her that I was in the process of trying to make the decision about whether or not to move to the West Coast and gave her my reasons while revealing the family distress over my possible relocation. She asked me many questions about every facet of my life, education, my goals, and my relationship with friends and family. On hindsight I realize she wanted to know more about me and in many ways, gauge my maturity level.

When we were winding down, she said the following, "I won't advise you to go or stay but, one thing I can tell you, if you want to grow as a human being, you have to go."

At that moment, a bell went off and my decision was finally made. Thank you, Mary.

WALKING ON AIR
MOMENT

I was born with what was then called a "lazy" eye, in other words, it simply had very poor vision. Added to that, it was crossed and rested very close to my nose. The result was that when I looked in the mirror, my left eye was looking directly at me and my right eye decidedly was not.

My parents were not the type to seek out the new surgery that was correcting this eye issue so I grew up with it, and since my left eye vision was excellent, I successfully adapted during grade school and high school. Was I occasionally called "cross eye" at school? Yes but again, I adapted.

I graduated from high school at 16 and by 17 I had a full-time job with health benefits and one of my first tasks was to seek out an eye surgeon who would straighten my way-ward eye. This effort paid off and after my first year of work I scheduled the surgery.

Surgery was completed, then a two day hospital stay, then home with a bandaged eye for about a week. During most of that week, every member of my family and friends reminded me on a daily basis to keep my hands off of the bandage. In other words, don't pull the bandage down to look at the eye. As anxious as I was to see the corrected eye, I waited patiently for the next surgeon's appointment.

I spent one of these days at my Grandmother's home and she decided to go to the grocery store. As soon as she left, I was alone in the house and seized at the opportunity to take a look. I went into an upstairs bedroom, closed the door, and stood in front of the mirror and carefully peeled away the bandage.

What I saw literally took my breath away. For the first time in my almost 18 years, both eyes were looking at me. I recall that I said in a whisper "wow" and continued to look at my eyes.

I was walking on air. What a moment of joy.

COMMITMENTS AND INTERESTS FOR ALL SEASONS

1. Charity - I just like the word but let there be no mistake about this, it is not financial charity I'm thinking about but the human extension of that day to day care of others. I believe the Catholics call it The Corporal Works of Mercy which includes feeding the hungry, water for the thirsty, clothes and housing, care for the sick, and compassion and care for the grieving and dying.

   In other words, take care of others. Be a volunteer. Remember the good people. and never forget a favor.

2. My Friends - As noted in Special People, over the years my friends became family and I never forget a favor and the people who were up close and personal. As I tell them frequently, they've got me whether they want me or not.

3. Pay It Forward - The opportunity to pay back many of the folks who have been so kind and generous with me doesn't always present itself. So I pay it forward by extending my assistance to others where needed. This is a very firm commitment.

4. Nobel Peace Prize - Imagine that some countries talk about peace, some countries have no idea what it is, religious people tout it, politicians use the word

with duplicity, and the man who invented dynamite established a singular, universal, non-politicized award in honor of those who truly seek peace at all levels.

I did a retrospective on this Prize and looked at every winner going back to the beginning. What a fascinating lesson in peace. I recommend this lesson for everyone.

5. United States Constitution - A fascinating document continually reviewed or adjusted or changed by the Supreme Court. Very glad to have it. So thankful I'm an American.

6. The Human Brain - How can one look at the complexity of that grey matter and what it does and not believe in God?

7. Sports - I have always been a sports fan, with very big interest in football, baseball and women's sports. Especially attached to World Series and Super Bowl. Both of my homes, the West Coast and Midwest, have occasional winners in these areas.

During one of my Seasons, I was the only female quarterback in our Sunday afternoon touch football games. Great fun and good for all since we all worked in offices—we were desk jockeys. The biggest problem with this was a very sore body on Monday morning.

This life time interest gave birth to my commitment to exercise and good physical health. Still do my treadmill walk and strength training every day.

SEASON THREE

WESTWARD HO

THE GREAT ESCAPE

TO

DIFFERENT IDEAS AND CULTURE,

VERY COSMOPOLITAN.

I'm getting it.

I'M GETTING IT!!

Think about this. I was now on the West Coast of the United States and just a twelve minute drive to take in the Pacific Ocean or a five minute drive to visit San Francisco Bay. Add to that I come home from work to a pleasant and happy environment and not one person wants to talk about my still being single. Folks, it doesn't get better than this.

Then add to that, I'm spending my 20s and most of my 30s in San Francisco. What an incredible time. It was an exciting period, a learning event, and a time of extraordinary growth which was and will always be close to my heart.

While I was always mature, this period turned me into a grown-up. It was so different, with so many changes in my "world", that I experienced great growth as a human being. My awareness of the importance of career, relationships, money and life's path were a constant factor in my choices and behaviors. If ever there was an example of how experiences and social culture shape relationships, behaviors, view of gender and sexuality, it would be at this point in my life. The merging of my maturity with so many differences gave birth to a different person. Did I give up my value system? No, but all of these experiences while contributing to my growth produced a mature person very comfortable with herself. It was a good place to be.

This very cosmopolitan city exploded around me with a world of music, theater, art, ideas and people of different cultures, religions, sexual orientations, and life paths. I lived in a guest house (a San Francisco fancy name for a boarding house) for a number of years with 50 residents representing 18 states and 5 countries. During this time, I was turned to learning—my brain was assimilating at warp speed and turning this information back out into behaviors, ideals, values and a wonderful view of myself and my life.

This San Francisco time gave me so much that it would fill an entire book if I try to put it all here but for your interests, here are some highlights. Many women and men who were important and close became the special people in my life and some were like family. Those friendships were sustaining and life long and were there for me.

My next growth was in the area of the arts specifically, opera, classical music and art. I literally got hooked on opera very early simply because I could afford a ticket even though my seat was high enough to give one a nose bleed, but that didn't matter, since it was really all about the voices and music. Some of the voices I was fortunate enough to hear were Marian Anderson, Jan Peerce, Giulietta Simionato, Robert Merrill and Rene Fleming. Absolutely breathtaking.

This growth in music appreciation also carried over to musical shows and concerts. Certainly, one that stands out was at the Presidio of San Francisco on July 4th, watching the fireworks across San Francisco Bay, the canons fired from the Presidio, as I listened to the U. S. Army Band play The Stars and Stripes Forever. Outstanding!

During this time, my work life was involved primarily with clerical tasks. Except for one position that had some challenging administrative work, I was usually doing clerical work designed for women, the consequence of which was making the necessary money while bored. This working time in my life started a long pursuit for equality for women and then for all minorities. I was internally cranky but somewhat quieter externally simply because I lacked that kind of experience. On occasion, however, I did have my say, sometimes successfully but more likely my verbosity precipitated a job change.

A big plus was having very good friends who recognized

my merry-go-round work life and referred me to the San Francisco School System for a series of intellectual and vocational tests. The result of this testing enhanced my confidence and at a very personal level put to rest a doubt about my intellect that had been given to me by a home life that focused more on the male of the species. I now had the necessary encouragement to start taking college courses. I attended several junior colleges and found the experience interesting and great fun.

Now, in my 30s and while greatly enjoying life, I was stopped in my tracks by two physical issues. I experienced a cervical spine fracture in an auto accident and a head injury/concussion in a home accident caused by crashing into a cabinet door because I was in a big hurry. This combination put the brakes on my life and activities and I was at home in recovery for over a year. As I was recovering, I returned to work on a part-time basis but frankly it takes time to recover physical and emotional balance after two serious accidents.

And then, along came my invitation from the Pacific Northwest.

Moving North..............................Before we leave SF, however, take a look at all the other pieces of information in this LIFE'S JOURNEY and TIMES AND CHANGE. Hope all readers enjoy and then, pack your bags and get ready to travel.

THE MAGNET OF MY MORAL COMPASS

Integrity is defined as adherence to a code of values or incorruptibility, or soundness, or completeness, or more simply, honesty; but however one looks at integrity, it becomes the behavioral dance of all of our lives.

Here is my dance.

It rules all. It is in my heart when I extend out to others; in my mind as I move along life's path; in my speech when I must take a stand; it is a reminder of who I am, and most of all, it is in my soul when I must answer to myself and be accountable.

Sometimes this magnet of my moral compass walks hand-in-hand with courage. In those complex moments when, regardless of the consequences, I must speak up in defense of another or provide information that has been omitted, I recognize the depth and sometimes frightening responsibility of doing the right thing. While remaining silent would not be verbally lying, I would have allowed my silence to have a voice

The fall out for all of us having made integrity the center piece of our value system is a certain calmness about our lives and a comfort in our own skin. Think about this, if you tell a lie, it might take ten lies to cover up and at that point will you remember what you said or didn't say? If you don't remember you might self-destruct. The truth is simply easier.

For everyone, trust and credibility are significant not only in how others view us but in how we view ourselves. In the final analysis, it will come down to our judgment, our morality, and our respect for ourselves and others. It is extremely important that we all be pleased with who we see in the mirror.

THE BIG TEST, which follows, takes a hard (and comical) look at this subject.

Keep in mind, it is much easier to go forward or fall back on a foundation of truth. In the vernacular of today, it's way cooler.

THE BIG TEST

So now you know how I feel about integrity. I believe it completely. It doesn't mean that we all won't be tested by some event in our lives. Here is mine.

I had accepted a temporary position doing my secretary thing in Los Angeles and while I was only going to be there for three or four months, I opened a checking account at the bank closest to my employment in the downtown area. Bear in mind that the timing for this particular position and temporary relocation was in the pre-computer days. Hence on payday, I would walk the three blocks to the bank to deposit my check.

I submitted my pay check, appropriately endorsed, along with the small book used in those days that indicated your deposits and totals. The young lady bank clerk checked my submissions, did her thing, and returned the small book to me. I left the bank and headed back to the office and for a reason I don't understand, I didn't immediately check the book to look at the deposit amount.

On my way back to the office, I opened the little book to take a look and was stopped in my tracks. The bank had deposited slightly over $23,000.00 to my account. I stood, without movement, mouth open, shock written on my face, in the middle of a block in downtown Los Angeles. I literally couldn't move for several minutes. Too bad I have no picture of the expression on my face when I discovered that large deposit—it would be a classic.

After regaining my composure, I headed back to the bank, still in shock but wondering what the heck happened. When

I presented the book to the teller, she looked a little flustered but said there was no problem. When I showed her the pay check stub which was for approximately $350.00, she turned white and I was concerned that she might faint. We talked briefly, she consulted with the bank officers and other tellers, and after about an hour, my deposit was corrected to reflect the proper amount.

What a day, what a moment, and frankly, I didn't have to weigh my options when I discovered the erroneous amount, it was an easy decision.

I still recall with clarity the moment when I looked at the deposit recorded in that book.

TALK ABOUT A SHOCK!!

INCREDIBLE MOMENT

It was a beautiful, sunny, San Francisco kind of day in the 1960s.

My contact lenses were bothering me as they were prone to do, so I left work just before lunchtime and hiked up Post Street to visit the "contact guy" for some adjustment.

I waited my turn, saw my eye guy, explained my problem, he removed my contacts and sent me back out to the waiting room. I decided to go outside and do some people and car watching or do as much watching as I could absent my plastic eyes.

No traffic on Post Street, very unusual. In my blur, I saw flashing lights further down Post and a blurry mass that I assumed was an accident of some sort since there was no moving traffic. I did some window shopping and when I looked down Post again, it appeared the flashing lights and mass were closer but there was still no moving traffic. I couldn't make out exactly what was going on but whatever it was, it was definitely moving my way.

I stepped off the curb and watched as this blurry mass with flashing lights approached. About a block or so away, I recognized a single car in front, a convertible, surrounded on either side by San Francisco police motorcycles.

About 50 feet or so from me I could see the people in the car, with one man standing and another holding his waist.

They were now directly in front of me and Bobby Kennedy leaned forward and shook my hand. I said "Good Luck, Senator." He replied "Thank You."

WOW!!

MY COMPANION

I could not have imagined such a relationship. We were so different—he was Jewish, of German ethnicity, and a Newark, New Jersey, street boy; I was Catholic, of Irish/German ethnicity, and a Midwestern home girl. We started dating in San Francisco and this journey continued for a number of years. In some incredible way we became a couple. What a surprise!

After our first six months, he decided to accept a contract job with a federal contractor on Guam. We parted well with some trepidation but I suspect both of us wondering "what if?" On a Saturday morning about three months later, he called and we chatted for about 15 minutes. At that point he inquired what I was going to do the rest of the day and I replied I had no plans. He asked in a calm voice if I had time to come to the airport and pick him up. After I mentally picked myself up off of the floor and found the phone, I said yes and this very nice romance continued.

Did we live together? No! Were we engaged? No! Did we have each other's back? Yes! And perhaps most important, were we committed? Very much so!

We enjoyed each other and had great conversations. I still had not returned to work following the accidents mentioned earlier, and he became a wonderful emotional supporter for me during a difficult time. After a year or so my opportunity to move to the Pacific Northwest came about and he fully supported the move since he felt it was an opportunity for me to get back on life's track. He followed that up by applying for and accepting a job in the Pacific Northwest so that we could continue our relationship. I moved north a few weeks after he did so we continued where we left off. Good to be in the same city again.

During the years in the Northwest, we enjoyed life together having mostly good times with a few stressful events thrown in. A few years later, I had to have a mastectomy which was not precipitated by an active malignancy but rather by a pre-cancerous condition. He was very helpful during the time I was making the decision and then was at the hospital 24/7 during surgery and several days after. In recovery, he picked me up every day on his way home from work and I spent the evening and night at his house. Talk about good care and having my back—-this was the best.

All went well in recovery and in life. Our closeness continued for the next five years for a total of nine years and it was a very good time for both of us and the relationship. We greatly enjoyed our time together which was joyful, caring, and loving. In addition to a good relationship, we both had jobs that we enjoyed, so all was well for both of us.

The good times were with us but as sometimes happens, we were changing. During the last year we were together, we both started moving in different directions in terms of our interests and particularly looking at the future. At that point in time, after much conversation and thought, we made a decision to separate and we parted feeling very grateful for our time together.

As I have said repeatedly, I have been gifted by the people in my life.

ALL MY WHEELS

When it comes to personal lifetime connections, it was not booze, sex, money, drugs, etc., it was my wheels. Can't get along without one. Currently, I'm on my 11th "last" car and my 41st overall. My first few were various colors but most have been red. Because it was all I could afford, for a period of time in San Francisco, I purchased very old junk cars from my friendly junk car dealer. They cost $85 each and when they broke down, usually about a year to eighteen months later, for $10 my dealer picked it up. I probably had 4 or 5 of these over a six year period of time. Here are two that were hilarious.

First, a 1940 Oldsmobile, four door, the size of a tank, and built with steel since plastic wasn't a part of our lives. It developed a tiny gas line leak so I would park it pointing down on one of the hills in my neighborhood. When I needed to go to the store, I released the brake and coasted down six blocks turning the motor on only when I was looking for a parking spot. I parked the car, did my shopping, or lunch, then drove to the nearest gas station and purchased 25 cents worth of gas, which at that time was almost a gallon. The funny man at the station always asked to see my quarter before pumping. I drove back up the hills and parked the car on the same hill facing downward. I was ready for tomorrow.

Second, I had a very old green Plymouth and while it was parked, another car hit the driver's side door and it needed to be replaced. I couldn't afford a new door so the repair people found a purple door for $7.00 and, with no painting, I had that put on the car. Good news; I could always find my car. Bad news; I got a lot of parking tickets.

Not to worry, folks, over the years I made enough money to purchase what I called "grown-up" cars, so voluntarily and happily left the junk car business.

Current car: 2019 Camry. Red, of course.

CLOSE CALL
- THE SECOND

In my mid-thirties, on my way to work, an Olds 88 rear ended my VW Bug. I could feel something happen to my neck but I had feeling in my legs so got out of the car, attended to the driver accident issues, and then went on to work.

Although the diagnosis came seven years later, I had broken my neck, specifically C3 and C4. When I was finally advised of this injury, the medical people were shocked since they said that only 1%, give or take, survive this injury and that small percentage are quadriplegics.

I walked away from my car.

The side effects of this injury have been long term and, in many ways, a life time experience. I've learned to deal with not only neck problems but back issues as well, since the initial impact moved my spinal column. When these neck and back issues are difficult, I always remind myself that I survived against the odds hence they become more manageable. And, I try to....................

LIVE LIFE FULLY

TIMES AND CHANGES

MLK IMPACT
FROM THE PERSPECTIVE OF A WHITE, LIBERAL FEMALE IN THE TIMES OF MARTIN LUTHER KING, JR.

I was living the fun life of a young person in a San Francisco, a cosmopolitan city that had introduced me to the opera, classical music, professional sports and art. I was comfortable and all was well with my world.

It was the 1960s and while I was not active in the civil rights movement, I could not escape its impact and the resulting changes albeit somewhat small at first.

And then along came Martin Luther King, Jr. who shook my complacency and naivete. He made me look away from myself and toward the rest of the world. He pointed out issues and problems that I was aware of but had been successful in ignoring. He hammered at the concept of equality until I could no longer look away. For me then, equality was no longer an idea with which I agreed but now had the added responsibility of being a moral choice. I had to leave my intellectual and emotional safe house.

Initially I became more involved in women's issues particularly as they applied to the concept of equal pay for equal work. From there it was an easy but sad journey to look at the disparity of business and career treatment of white women and men versus Black and Hispanic employees. The difference was shocking. I campaigned for pro-equality candidates for office and made my voice heard in the workplace. I was finally aware and I got involved.

This was the ripple effect that MLK had on me.

DIVERSITY'S BIG THREE

The word diversity is huge—it marches down such a wide path. The following three are a small but significant indicator of my road to and learning from the experience of diversity. The fact that I remember each one after so many years says much about their influence on my life.

The First: I grew up in a home sometimes overwhelmed by an alcoholic, my Father. He was born at the end of the nineteenth century and was a standard, bigoted, good-old-boy connected to that time. His bigotry was most often directed at African Americans which produced language that was racially inappropriate and very unkind. By the time I was in high school, I was one disgusted twelve year old. I came to the conclusion that if he said people of color were bad, then they must be good people. After that I made a small but dedicated effort to learn more and then always reminded myself that we are all equal.

The Second - San Francisco: One of my temporary positions was as a secretary to a Senior Executive with a large investment firm. In their human resources discussions, diversity specifically the large Mexican/Catholic population in the city, came up often. As a result of this, a supervisor in my division hired a 26 year old American of Mexican ethnicity. He was a very pleasant person but with critically limited experience and education needed for his job. He did not last long and was let go since he could not meet the expectations of his position. The attitude in and out of the executive offices was along the lines of "they" simply can't do this kind of work. Bottom line: this was a set-up. He was hired to fail and support a strategy of veiled discrimination. This was the first time I had seen this behavior up close and personal. I was annoyed and after sharing that feeling with my supervisor (Executive V.P.), I was removed from this firm and transferred to another without explanation.

The Third - San Francisco: I worked for a Senior Scientist as an Administrative Assistant in a large engineering firm. During this time, the gay community both men and women, were significantly large but still in the closet. While there were probably many gays employed at my firm, everyone played "lets pretend" and assumed that most sexual orientation was heterosexual. The exception was Ben, a twenty year old who worked in the mail room, and while he didn't broadcast his orientation, many of us were aware and frankly liked him, gay or straight because he was a very good person. We all felt that his sexual orientation was none of our business. On a particular Monday, one of my colleagues advised that Ben had been murdered over the weekend by the gay bashers. They beat him severely, placed his body on the streetcar tracks and he was run over. After my recovery from much anger and grief, I made a silent commitment to learn more about gay people and their lives. This was made easy for me since a good female friend of mine acknowledged that she too was gay. I hadn't known but she was my introduction to the gay community. I became their "straight" friend and I'm pleased to say after all these years, a few of us are still in touch. Along with many of my colleagues, we registered formal and not-so-formal complaints with the law enforcement community regarding Ben.

Conclusion:

These were excellent learning experiences and I was up close and personal for all three. They proved to be a thoughtful guidance during my career in San Francisco, Pacific Northwest and the Midwest.

Their life long effect on me has been a commitment to diversity and a strong belief that we are all created equal in the eyes of God and before the law.

SEASON FOUR

NORTHWARD BOUND

NEW FAMILY,

FRESH PERSPECTIVE,

GROWING.

Great Change

GREAT CHANGE

Once again, I was blessed by having friends who reached out. They were in Portland, Oregon, and invited me to come up and stay with them. This was extraordinary. A Mom and Dad with three little girls offered me a place to stay as I finished recovering from my accidents. I became a member of this family so the blessing for me was that I experienced being a full family member with all the unconditional good stuff that went with it. There was no problem or criticism connected with my gender, marital status, desire to continue my education, and wanting to do something other than being a secretary. I was accepted and loved for who I was and my thoughts and plans for the present and future. This was a time of growth and healing.

I was encouraged to see a local psychologist to clear up the emotional side effects of the accidents and it also had the gratifying result of putting to rest and in perspective my somewhat chaotic home life growing up. I was very fortunate and successful.

My anticipated short time in Portland turned into relocating and signing on with a temp agency to do clerical work which paid the bills while I got settled. Additionally, I returned to school taking a variety of classes at local colleges. From the beginning, I hadn't planned on staying in Portland, but it turned out to be a great move and very beneficial job wise. Frankly, I lucked out.

Part of that good luck was being asked to fill in at a clinical psychologist's office. I started by managing the office and the phone and anything else that needed to be done and then administered the psychological and intellectual tests that were frequently needed. This effort and dealing with the patients helped me find my vocational gift—I was finally where I belonged. Over the next five years, the job grew and in addition to office management and test administration, and after considerable training and a number of psychology classes at a local college, I was involved in test evaluations, home evaluations and taking emergency calls in the psychologist's absence.

My total time working for clinical psychologists in the mental health field was ten years and this experience set the stage for future career growth. It provided excellent experience in working with people problems in any business environment. I had a gift and it was revealed at this time.

I honestly believed that I would not be suited to living in any place but San Francisco. Not so! Living in Portland was a growing, learning, and very good period of time. My good friends had become my second family and I was given the opportunity to grow intellectually and emotionally.

Did I miss California? Yes, but frankly my life took on a more successful and stable path, one that had good emotional and career direction. My career as noted above was finally interesting and stable. Then, I had a group of friends, mostly women, with whom I would socialize. Actually, several of us got together for dinner every month, a different person hosted at her home, and the rest of us brought part of the dinner. We were different ages, had varying careers, with most being single, and all these differences made for very interesting and sometimes very funny conversations. Another plus factor was that we all took good care for one another when needed. You can see that this entire time, even with some physical issues, was successful and happy.

Overall, my time in Portland was good with a glitch now and then. My writings in this Season reflect the good which was most of the time, and the one big problem was more manageable because I was in the right place at the right time. I continued my educational pursuits at the local community college and, as much as possible, concentrated on psychological and mental health studies. As mentioned before, mental health and human behavior became my focus and strong learning areas.

After many good years in Portland, I took a hard look at my career and my life as I was getting a little older and started occasionally reflecting on the future which included retirement. This thinking started some planning on my part and prompted me to accept a position with the Federal Civil Service working in the Human Resources/Employee Relations area. I remained with the Federal Service in that field of endeavor for many more years when for family considerations, I made the decision to move back to the Midwest.

Before we leave, however, read more about and enjoy the Northward Bound experience. Then, we need to pack again.

WHAT A FAMILY!

So, I was recovering in beautiful San Francisco and during this time, I kept in touch with several West Coast friends namely Eva and Arny in the Pacific Northwest. Eva and I met in San Francisco and became good friends which was amazing since we were from different family backgrounds, different religious affiliations, and different educational levels. Somehow all those differences connected and a life time friendship was born. What a blessing for me.

Eva married Arny and they remained in San Fran for a while and during this time Arny referred me to the San Francisco School Board for testing the results of which opened my eyes and my thinking to more options in the work world.

Then they moved to the Pacific Northwest and started having baby girls—three to be exact over the next ten years. So here they are, a Mom and Dad, and a 6 year old, a 9 year old, and an 11 year old, and Eva called me one evening and said that she and Arny had discussed my situation in San Francisco and thought I should come up and stay with them. I accepted and the second day I was living with them, Arny told me that I had bed and board as long as I needed it. Am I not very fortunate?

Everything about that move provided the change and opportunities needed to move on with my life. As previously mentioned I saw a psychologist and was finally able to put to rest the problems associated with the accidents and my somewhat difficult life while growing up. Then the opportunity to work in the mental health field for ten years moved my career in a challenging direction—in other words, I was no longer bored.

Taking it one step further, after much thought and consideration, I finally connected with the Federal Civil Service and which led to more challenging work not to mention remuneration. This move proved to be a great choice in that it set me up for future work in employee relations and started an excellent path for retirement. And, all this came about because two friends stepped up to the plate and took a chance and filled in the family gap for a friend.

Not unlike my friend Marsha in my early life, Eva and Arny provided the direction and encouragement and family base that moved me forward. In addition to that, it has been a life time connection not only with Eva and Arny but with three little girls. I watched them grow up and they now have families of their own. What fun!

Let me introduce you to:

Lise, the oldest, was very smart, very verbal, and marched to a different drummer as I did hence our connection. We had some very funny moments. She was my challenge.

Andrea arrived in the world a few years later and, again, what a fun person. Another smarty, who frequently took my side in discussions, and gave up her room for me when I arrived. She was my bud.

Karin, the baby, became my pal because, according to her, "you're the one who took me to all those crappy movies." We are still in touch, still laughing. My third gift.

As you can see, this family became my family. It doesn't get better than this. Once again, I go back to the song WIND BENEATH MY WINGS and the question from that song that resonates from me to all five members of this family.

I ask, "Did you ever know that you're my heroes?"

CHOOSE LIFE

There are big things and smaller things to review, evaluate, focus on, research, and make a decision and while this one was emotional and difficult, it turned out for the best with no enduring sad times. As a matter of fact, after the solution was taken care of, my life was happier, more relaxed and more joyful than ever. I cover it here and do so hoping that it might be of some assistance to other women if they are faced with this situation.

In my late twenties, I developed a fibrous cystic disease in both breasts. They were treated and the lumps looked at by specialists in that field and all was well for a number of years. By my mid-thirties, the disease was becoming more aggressive and more difficult. I had an occasional abscess and a couple of biopsies. Still, all was managed well with no interference in my daily life and that continued through and well after my move to the Pacific Northwest.

As noted previously, my life in general settled very nicely after the move and between good friends, my significant other (SO), and my job working with psychologists, all was well. The disease stabilized for several years and I was hopeful that it would remain in that condition. Unfortunately, it became aggressive again and I started what was now a familiar process of seeing specialists and having CTs. For a while, I operated under the belief that it would stabilize and I continued on with my life. While there was an occasional problem, my life was good and joyful.

Finally, the problem accelerated and I went from having a couple of abscesses a year to having a couple a month and the specialists advised that they could no longer tell one lump from another which made diagnosis very difficult and risky. At this point, with my professional advisors concurring, I had to consider a mastectomy. It was a tough decision to make since I did not have an active cancer but I was at some risk. Knowing and understanding the risk, I then moved ahead for several months while I did as much research as possible on the medical options and I also saw four different specialists seeking advice. My coverage of the emotional side of this was having many conversations and good advice with those up close and personal in my life. I made my decision and the surgery was scheduled.

It wasn't all anxiety and gloom, let me tell you about a great laugh I had with one of the specialists. It was determined by the specialists that I should have implants because I am a small person and there was concern that my skin rubbing against my rib cage would cause abrasions. Size was never a priority for me but I didn't want to follow up surgery with another problem. While seeing one of the specialists for advice, I told him that I had never considered being bigger, but out of curiosity, how big did implants come? I remember his response word for word. "Let me think. OK, they are all the way from you to Oh My God." I still laugh out loud when I remember that comment.

The surgery went well and after a week in the hospital, I went home. Actually, I was at two different homes. My SO picked me up at my home every evening on his way home from work. I had dinner and spent the evening and night with him and then on his way to work the next morning, he dropped me at my home to spend the day. We kept this back and forth for a couple of weeks until I was ready to accomplish more. Because of the implants I was somewhat restricted in what I could get done so this care was physically and emotionally healing.

I returned to work on a shortened schedule and then back

to full time after a few more weeks. I felt great and was delighted that this problem that had been hanging over my head was finally put to rest. The biopsy from surgery indicated two areas of pre-cancerous tissue. I asked how long before an active malignancy would have manifested, and they replied three to four years. My sigh of relief was, and remains, deep.

Looking at this entire issue from early problems to the surgery, I determined that the most difficulty came from making the decision to go forward. Let me share one of the ideas or suggestions that was paramount in making my decision.

Two words popped up in a conversation with a friend. They were—CHOOSE LIFE. I did and with it all, what a beautiful choice it has been.

FUN STUFF

In the month or so prior to having the mastectomy, I told everyone in my life that I didn't want to be overloaded with the "poor Bryn" or "poor baby" routine since I felt it would not be helpful and make my emotional decision more difficult.

My friends accommodated by bringing presents to our monthly dinner just before surgery. It was called a "boob shower."

A wonderful idea. There was much laughter.

STRICTLY BUSINESS

THE UNCONVENTIONAL WISDOM OF SUCCESS

I have spent most of my adult life working in both the private and public sectors and I don't think I have an action plan left in me. What I do have, however, are some "tips" on how one might move ahead, stay out of trouble or at least enjoy themselves. We all understand the obvious success traits such as intelligence and education but I've had the time to develop the not so apparent and offer them now. So, let's assume that after your undergraduate and graduate (if possible) degrees, you've done your time in the trenches, paid your dues and now feel you're ready to be seriously considered to move upward and onward. Understanding what I've come to call, The Big Four, may offer some unconventional insights to assist you as you participate in the corporate dance, with or without your tap shoes.

The Big Four

1. Know Your Audience

2. Politics and Protocol

3. Rules of Engagement or Watch Your Timing

4. Being sneaky is not all bad.

Know Your Audience

Q: Who is your audience? A: Everyone. Your supervisor, your chain of command, colleagues, the IT staff, human resources, financial types, sales, marketing, security, etc., etc., etc.

Where I find people making their biggest mistake as it relates to their audience is, assuming that when it comes to their own basic attitude and method of operation (M.O.), one size fits all. It does not. For instance, what do you know about your immediate supervisor or team leader or branch chief or division director? I know, I know, you work for them and do what you're told. Other than that, do you know them as people? I'm not suggesting social relationship but rather paying close attention to their work style as much as the presenting business front and when given the opportunity, look at the human side.

Suppose your boss, who makes your assignments and, for the moment, controls your work life, is detail oriented, maybe she/he is a stickler for being on time, or is a bureaucrat, or is laid back about work, or has a rigid work style, or has many other work style personality traits, it is in your best interest to pay attention and find out who you're working for and with. This may seem very basic but it is amazing how many times people just go with their past M.O., whether it fits or not, and keep butting their heads against the same wall. Don't misunderstand, I'm not talking about always doing things the same way or dampening creativity, but rather acknowledging the differences and meshing the work preferences. Learn to be flexible and adaptable—it has career enhancing potential.

So, if you're going to suggest a new process or procedure, do so after you sit back, take a look, learn, listen, watch, ask questions, and put your finger on the work style pulse. If you do this, you may finally know your audience and trust me when I tell you that your audience just might know you.

If this idea somewhat political? Yes indeed, which leads us to . . . .

Politics and Protocol

Q: What is Politics? A: The art or science of guiding or influencing policy.

Politics is not confined to the government. Every large or small organization has its own variation on how politics are played out in their organization and it is the diversity of this gamesmanship that makes each political menu so different. If you are new to an organization or division or department, never assume that what you experienced before will continue. Make it a point to learn and be aware of the political landscape.

A word of advice, don't get caught up in political gossip. Staff members who are involved in the gossip machine usually lack credibility and, in my experience, aren't taken seriously.

Q: What is Protocol? A: Rules governing occasions and/or accepted behavior in a situation.

I discovered that many young people, just out of college, have a tendency to believe that they know protocol and based on that belief, they use the same method of operation they've used in their limited past. So, for these very bright and inexperienced people and for anyone a long way from college who still doesn't "get it", here are but a few simple but basic protocols to observe.

- You want to talk to someone on your staff who is already engaged in a conversation. Don't move in close and stare at both parties. This causes great annoyance and makes you look like a twelve year old. If there is an emergency, excuse yourself and interrupt. Otherwise back off and wait until they have finished.

- Even without a dress code, learn how to dress. The working world we live in is much more casual than in the past but dress in at least a sporty/casual style. In other words, don't look like you were cleaning out the garage when you remembered you should come to work. I've seen colleagues lose opportunities or travel or attend conferences because management was concerned about how they would dress.

- When it comes to having work related discussions with no emergency involved, don't bypass your immediate supervisor. Maybe your boss is in a meeting or won't be in the office until the next day, if you elevate your conversation to your second level supervisor, be sure of your ground. In other words, don't step on your supervisor's toes—be wise.

These three protocols are but a drop in the bucket of the information in order to tread smartly at work. Some people think protocol is another way to describe having manners, but to put it succinctly, use common sense. If you don't have common sense, find someone who does.

Moving along, while you're learning to be politically correct and protocol conscious, you might want to learn about the . . . .

Rules of Engagement and Watch Your Timing

Q: What is an Engagement? A: To connect or interlock with.
Q: What is Timing? A: To set the tempo.

In a place where I worked years ago, I established certain rules of engagement when it came to individual meetings with our supervisor, scheduling meetings, or for that matter, scheduling social events at work. In those rules, timing was one of the critical issues since I'm a firm believer in the concept that timing bears considerable weight in the outcome of many endeavors.

Perhaps one of your most important engagements will be discussions with your supervisor, the one-on-one kind of meeting. Next would be staff or project meetings to talk business. So, for these engagements, I suggest the following rules:

1. Don't go after your boss before she or he has their coat off. Give them time to settle.

2. Never, I repeat, never schedule a meeting or drop in on your boss just before lunch. It is more probable than not that she/he will have low B.S. (blood sugar) and might be crabby. Low B.S. creates a tenseness and if you are asking for something, you're more likely to get a "no" at this time of day. If your boss does not eat breakfast (if you know your audience, you should know this), be especially careful of your timing. How to manage this no breakfast issue is covered under Surreptitious/Sneaky.

3. If you're going to ask your boss for a raise, or career assistance, or time off, do your homework and be prepared. Make a good case for why you should have what you're asking for and have a formal written proposal. Be professional.

4. Schedule group meetings before 11:00 AM or Between 1:00 PM and 3:00 PM. The participants are not as likely to be tired or cranky.

Again, these are just a few examples of rules of engagement. The best advice I've ever received pertaining to these engagement rules is to try and approach management types using skill and good timing. Someone told me once "just because you're in a great mood, doesn't mean others are, so be calm and approach carefully". This advice has served me well. And where does all this lead you? Down the path of . . . .
. . . .

Being Surreptitious/Sneaky Isn't All Bad

Q: What is surreptitious or sneaky? A: Done, made or acquired by stealth.

Stealth is defined as secret or unobtrusive and unobtrusive is defined as inconspicuous, and I define this process as getting something done quietly and behind the scenes. Now I don't mean sneaky or stab in the back or blind siding that becomes harmful or mean, since those have no place in your life let alone in your career. Sometimes, however, the direct and appropriate in-your-face approach just won't get the job done and surreptitious behavior might be more effective. As an example and referring back to Rules of Engagement and Timing, if you must visit with your boss just before lunch, consider taking a couple of cookies and put one on a napkin and slide it over to your supervisor. I personally have found chocolate chip cookies to be excellent anti-crabby devices.

The decision to use stealth and be unobtrusive while working on a particular project has some risks, the largest of which is stepping over the line of your own integrity. By no means should anyone confuse surreptitious behavior that is positive and productive with that same behavior that could be damaging. Watch your step—it is a very fine line.

In my career, I have faced situations where solving a problem or addressing an issue would be more successful if I operated unobtrusively. The skill is in knowing when to be direct and up front and when to operate in the background and making this distinction is, in large measure, a matter of intuition. Add to that intuition the following: your ability to know your audience; your skill in understanding politics and protocol; your smart use of practical rules of engagement; your thoughtful consideration of timing; and as noted above, staying ethical and operating with integrity.

Epilogue

As basic as these ideas are, there might be a tendency to ignore them. Did the Big Four assist me in my career? Yes, and I firmly believe that using these ideas can be very helpful.

When I say be wise in your working life, I mean it. This business of having a successful career really is as much a matter of personal behaviors and people skills as it is business acumen.

Don't forget that the quality of your personal and business life is your gift to yourself. It really is all up to you.

Good Luck and Godspeed.

GLASS CEILING?

Get Serious!

There really is such a thing as a glass ceiling. I worked in a building wherein one half was covered by a glass atrium and here is what I noticed. First, we had more sunlight, our actions were illuminated. Second, it was more open, giving the feeling that we weren't worried about being seen nor did we work in the shadows. Third, when the snow slid down the side of the atrium, the ensuing noise sounded like the rumble of God Almighty speaking to all of us about ethics, staying focused, humanity, etc. This was the real thing—a literal glass ceiling. Certainly not to be confused with the invisible barrier.

Now, as one manipulates this very real ceiling into a mental image that has significant meaning in the work world of women, it takes on new and meaningful descriptions. I would define it as an artificial barrier that prevents qualified women and minorities from advancing within an organization. If in her upwardly mobile work life a woman cannot get through this ceiling, then her career is frequently stalled at whatever level she holds as she gets within range. Realistically, what is the big deal about this ceiling? Why does it matter so much? Very simply, the passage through this imaginary ceiling propels her on the path of recognition and privilege not to mention the big three of business—money, power and prestige.

After we dissect all the reasons for women's difficulties in getting through the glass ceiling, a standout reason is a fear, in the hearts and minds of many, of placing in a woman's hands the great seducer in life, that being power. Nothing seduces like power, not money and not sex. I have seen this seduction up close and am constantly amazed by the changes wrought by this kind of authority. Bear in mind that it is not only the real ownership of power that is so attractive but the perception of power as well. Think about this, if you truly have power you are indeed the 1000 pound gorilla who sits wherever he or she wants. If you only think you have power, you are the baby chimp running around bumping into everything, but that perception is no less seductive.

At the core of many modern and not-so-modern masculine and some feminine beings, there rests a fear of a woman with power. It goes against the grain and the natural order of things. It is my belief that the discomfort experienced with the idea of a woman with power keeps the good old boys and girls holding down the glass ceiling.

As mentioned above, it is not exclusively a male prerogative. The answer is more complex, it is the Queen Bee Syndrome. There may be more than one reason for this but we must remember that most, but not all, women were not brought up learning from the team concept, the result of which might lend to an absence of support for their sisters. What I've witnessed with some successful females is that if they don't use their power and prestige to bring along other women, they stand mute and that might block the ceiling door. Sadly, what this really comes down to is that women don't always take very good care of each other in the work place.

There is a very select group of women who do a much better job of fostering inclusiveness and supporting one another. They are women-of-color. During my working years, I've always been aware that, while they are serious about their individual careers, they also focus on their community and their sisters-of-color. I've seen some of my African American friends who reached management levels make efforts to support and encourage, not only their African American sisters, but all women. They think and act more collectively with a payoff that puts a few more women through the magic ceiling.

Along the way, I have taken a hard look at the themes, theories and therapies of a variety of feminisms. I've digested liberal, radical, cultural, women-of-color, postmodernism, global/internationalism, lesbian/queer, and third-wave feminisms and the good news is that I've come away from this experience enlightened, encouraged and proud of these women who do and have done all that work so that I could have a career. I am in their debt.

In conclusion, we can talk and write about feminist themes and theories until our hands freeze and our voices fail. Think about this, however, we can spout about equal pay, gender bias, etc. but frankly, it lacks credibility if we do not take care of one another whether we are Women-Of-Color or Caucasian, Chicana or Asian, straight or lesbian, old or young, married or single or any combination thereof.

Gentlemen and Ladies of the world, I encourage you to step up to the plate and open the ceiling door and keep it open. The time is now.

SEASON FIVE

MY U-TURN
BACK TO THE MIDWEST

CAREER AND FINANCES

AND HOME

This is good.

THIS IS GOOD

OK, so I packed up, hired a storage facility, then movers, and hightailed it back to the Midwest without a job or living space of my own. This would have been an adventure had I not done all these things many years ago when I escaped to San Francisco. I would be staying with a relative for a while and felt that the job situation would probably work itself out since I now had Career Status with the Federal system.

Did the Feds let me down? No way. I hired on, in Human Resources, with a series of temporary federal appointments. They were located all over the area with a variety of federal agencies and, even though they were not permanent appointments, it was interesting and gave me a chance to get acquainted with the Midwest once again. Then a great and lucky moment. One of the temporary jobs needed a full-time, permanent, experienced person in HR and here I was. I was the right person, at the right time, with the right skills and experience.

A little clarity here is important. The family home life issues that drove me away from the Midwest many years ago were only occasionally a problem and add to that, I am an older and wiser and a much more independent person which lends itself to mature resolutions.

Now let's just move ahead a few years when I was living in my own apartment and had a fulltime permanent position in the Employee Relations (ER) part of Human Resources. As we all know, ER had become my strong suit and the years in mental health backed up my decisions. My working world was interesting, occasionally fun with a little social work thrown in the mix. When I took this job I was asked how I would feel being called a name if someone was angry. My answer was easy in that after ten years in mental health I felt there was no name I had not been called—I'm cool with all.

I worked with a bright, well educated, knowledgeable group who made it interesting. Actually, it was a good group who together provided a good environment. So my work time is involved with listening to problems from management and subordinates and then investigating problems and complaints and referring my findings to managers, employees and, if necessary, the attorneys. Then the occasional advice or assistance to employees needing some guidance, not only at work, but in their personal life.

After 9/11, the job took on considerable depth since I was in charge of Prevention of Violence in the Work Place and this involved writing the policy, managing the program, and taking on the role of primary fact-finder investigator. The next six years were eventful as we established a Risk Evaluation Team, and a series of policies and protocols to deal with this completely new mindset in the office world. This was a government wide challenge that brought with it different ideas and concepts on what was or was not acceptable behavior in a working environment. One welcome change was that bullying and angry language were considered acts of violence and no longer tolerated. These were long overdue but much needed behavioral adjustments.

Now we take it away from work and look at the other aspects of living, once again, in the Midwest. A part of this adventure is going through the adjustments required by moving from one culture to another, however, this social change from West Coast to Midwest was more difficult than the reverse. For instance, the Midwest is somewhat more conservative hence for middle age females, it was socially more difficult and being a little more outspoken on any number of issues could be another social deterrent. It was and has been a little frustrating and my hope is that the younger generation in the Midwest is smarter and more up to date.

One nice thing about this time of life is it allows me to benefit from the past, concentrate on and have fun in the present, and plan for the future. Once again, I'm wondering if I've done enough for others and then planning to do more. I spend my time being happy, joyful, having fun, investing emotionally in my relationships, and engaging in charitable endeavors. I was back to taking occasional classes at local colleges and finding, as I did before, that I was a learning junkie and school really enriched my life.

My away from work endeavors involve working with the hearing impaired, giving talks about hearing issues, and trying to find a way to assist the elderly poor in getting hearing aids. Now when I give talks or advise people on this subject can anyone doubt my expertise since I've been losing my audio gift for many years and had a cochlear implant in 2004. This work continues.

After you read this Season's writings that tell all, then we'll head into the next Season for a very different life: retirement and school. Read on and have fun with me.

THE CULTURE OF EVEN NUMBERS
MARRIED? SINGLE?
WHATEVER?

So I walk into the room where there are many people, mostly female, and after introductions it starts like this. Are you married? Single? Divorced? Have you ever been married? Do you plan on getting married? Do you have a boyfriend? Are you living with someone? And the questions go on and on ad nauseum. I answer politely with a yes or no while my internal answering machine is saying "who cares?"

If this behavior was an isolated or infrequent moment in time, we could stop right now. Since it isn't, you better read on.

One of the advantages of moving around this country and living in different areas is that you become aware that every large urban area has its own culture. Some of the differences and similarities are frequently obvious and "in your face" while others are subtle and at the same time very personal.

What we perceive and process is often determined by our age, gender, marital status, job, family background and the choices we make. Since I've lived in four good sized metropolitan areas, all over one million per, I've come to the conclusion that my singlehood (straight, not gay), my age and being of the female persuasion have the greatest impact on how I'm socially treated by others. This discovery seemed to be, in large measure, controlled by the social culture of the area where I was living and that culture's view of my (or anyone's) marital status.

California living which I enjoyed for so long was an open and easy lifestyle. As far as my female friends were concerned, my marital status didn't seem to matter—-I was accepted as a whole and competent person with or without a mate. In my years in the Pacific Northwest, while somewhat more conservative, women assumed in large measure that I possessed all the necessary attributes of a fully functioning and competent human being even though I was single.

Now we go to the Midwest. I returned here after my 30 plus years on the West Coast and what a difference in culture. Some call this a Bible Belt culture—I'm not sure about that since I'm unwilling to blame the Bible for what is a social culture. One thing I'm sure about is that being single, female and over 55 in this area is difficult and confounding to the female of the species.

Marital status is primary and if you have remained single for whatever the reason, you are definitely the low woman on the cultural and social scale. It is probably the most discrimination I've experienced in my entire life and what is most interesting is that it is, for the most part, without malice.

Let me give you some examples of what it's like to be single and middle aged in this geographical area. These examples are mine and mine alone but in interviewing many single women, there is a commonality of thought and experiences.

First, the issue of competency. There seems to be some doubt, especially in the eyes of married women, that a middle-aged, single women can act competently. I was asked by a charitable group to manage a silent auction for their annual fund-raising event. This is a very big job requiring letters to people and firms; managing and pricing all donations; designing all auction bid documents; physically setting up the auction area; and anything else that comes up in this process.

During this planning stage, I had coffee one morning with some of the people involved in the entire event. They asked many questions as I tried to fill them in on the auction process. As I walked away from the group, I heard one of the women who is about my age ask the others regarding me, "I wonder why they selected her to run the auction, she's never even been married?" Make any sense??

Second, while living out West, a part of my social life was involved with my married friends. A frequent (about once a month) occurrence was an invitation to dine with married friends in their home, just the three of us. On the other hand, since my return to the Midwest many years ago, I've been invited to a married couple's home on only five occasions. It doesn't seem to occur to a married couple to invite one of their single female friends. The only exception to this is when they invite my entire family, then I'm invited but never by myself.

Third and this is the most perplexing. These women are good, caring people who will always help out and do the right thing, however, they simply don't seem comfortable with having a single person in their house unless it is with a group.

So, there you have it—a somewhat meager social life that is the casualty of a geographical culture that says, with no factual support, that you are somewhat less competent or acceptable if you did not marry, have children, raise children, or run a household. A loss for all of us, married or single.

How to get around this culture? Establish a personal social life of friends from work or other sources. Participate in a variety of volunteer, educational and church functions. Take a class or classes at your local college or university. In other words, get involved.

Other than all that, on a daily basis, stay busy, have fun, have some chocolate AND don't forget to do something silly.

MEETING LIFE'S
BIG AUDIO
CHANGE

Changes or challenges? Either way, at a certain time or age in this journey, we all travel a road that is slow or fast but definitely makes us take a good look at our ability to adapt and then move on. This account marks the beginning of a life long challenge that has tested my patience and tenacity and attitude to never give up despite the hurdles.

In my late 30s I had my first indication that my audio world was slipping. My hearing seemed fine but my directional hearing was becoming difficult. If you called my name and I heard it, I may not know where the sound was coming from so I would do a complete 360 to locate the caller. At work, this happened often enough that a new sign was put on my desk. It read "The 360 Woman." Yes, a fun gift.

From that beginning, the progression was sort of slow but left no doubt that I was in for a reduction of hearing. Initial medical testing offered no answers as to why I would lose some hearing at such an early age. I was in for a wait and see game but as long as I could handle my work and phones, it was a manageable situation.

A nice ending to the above would be that my hearing remained acceptable but no such luck. My loss went from directional only to a high frequency problem and as time went along, phones became more difficult. Fortunately, I was able to secure special phones both at home and at work and I will say that while communication was a little more challenging, life moved along with only a small amount of adjustment.

I was fortunate in that from the first indication of an audio problem, the loss moved at a rather slow pace. In my 50s I finally got hearing aids. They were great and helped immensely. At this point, while challenging, the problem was well managed. Throughout this time, there was no definitive cause that accounted for this loss. The diagnosis came later—the Pacific Northwest physicians diagnosed Meniere's Disease, a disease that is usually accompanied by a balance problem. The hearing treatment continued as scheduled and the balance treatment has been effectively managed with only occasional moments where I walk like someone who has had a few too many martinis.

Fortunately, I was able to continue working and the next hearing crisis came in 2002 with a dramatic loss over three months. In my right ear, I went from 44% to 4%. It was a nerve-racking experience in that every day was different and I had no idea what was happening. Of course, I saw the otologist after about six weeks and while I was given the diagnosis of "sudden loss", I had no way of knowing when or if this decline would stop. The loss finally tapered off at about three months but it was severe enough to prompt more serious planning.

After this, my life with a more severe hearing loss, became somewhat difficult both at home and work. I researched all my options and made my decision, a Cochlear Implant. The process began and fortunately my otologist was one of the specialists in this field. It was 18 months of testing, discussions with other physicians, clearances with insurance companies, and many, many hours of internal review with myself.

Finally, all was ready with all decisions regarding equipment, which hospital, being away from work, care after surgery, etc. and the deed was done in March, 2004. Very successful surgery, easy recovery, and although we thought there might be a balance problem, there was not. I was at home for a week then back to work while I waited out the healing process and the equipment hook-up.

Hook-up day seemed like a miracle. The equipment was in place and I could hear out of that ear in a clear and specific way. It took some time getting accustomed to it because sounds were different for a while. For instance, voices sounded different and for a long time all voices for the first ten or fifteen minutes of each day sounded like Mickey Mouse or Donald Duck. You can appreciate that this became a fun issue at work since the staff wondered if they should only bring up difficult matters when they were Mickey or Donald. I always replied by suggesting that most of what they had to say was pretty much Mickey Mouse anyway. I did have some fun with it.

Going forward from this miracle, all was good for many years. Unfortunately, as I was entering a Masters Program, I had another sudden loss in the other ear, going from 60% to 10% in three months. Having a cochlear in one ear kept me working and in school and while we discussed another cochlear, I declined. While losing the hearing in this ear was difficult since it since it was my phone ear, I first tried the phone on the ear with the cochlear and when that wasn't successful, I got a captioned phone and have used one fairly successfully ever since. When using this phone, however, two things are absolutely required, a lot of patience and a great sense of humor. Occasionally and sometimes frequently, some of the captions are hilarious. As with everything else in the hearing journey, patience and adaptability make it work.

That is where we are today and I've turned all this knowledge and information into a no-charge presentation that I give with power point, to various business and church groups, nursing homes and do private counseling where needed. This presentation looks at the practical side of dealing with hearing loss, either your own or a family member or a colleague or a good friend.

Thank you for being here and take care of your hearing.

ONCE IN A LIFETIME

ITALY - 2006

A once in a lifetime trip and my only overseas journey. Nine days via plane and bus and traveling with a wonderful and fun group. The group included twenty-two members of a Catholic Diocese, seven members of the clergy including two Bishops, three Monsignors, two other parish priests, and, certainly last but not least my cousin from Texas. We all flew into Rome and spent a few days sightseeing and being in awe. After that, we boarded our bus and spent the next eight days traveling up and then down the boot. What a ride and here are the highlights.

ROME - What a city, like no other, and an incredible view at every turn. It took my breath away just realizing where I was.

VATICAN CITY - Amazing place. First, attended the Wednesday outdoor Papal audience held in St. Peter's Square. Because we were traveling with some of the clergy, we were sitting up close to the Pope and could view the crowd in the square. It was not a day of celebration or church Holy Day but there were approximately 12,000 people in the square. Awesome!

Second, I spent an hour or so in the Sistine Chapel. To walk around this very old room, stopping to stare at the ceiling to visually absorb Michel Angelo's work was truly breath taking. Another Walking On Air moment.

Finally, took a tour of other areas such as the art gallery and some of the other dedications to previous Popes and Saints. Incredible moment in time for me.

VENICE - What a place—-like no other. Had to take a boat ride just to get there. When I left a restaurant in the late evening, guess what? It was very quiet outside. Remember, no cars or traffic, hence no noise. It took a few moments to figure that out.

FLORENCE - City of Treasures. Took in the art of Fra Angelico. Extraordinary.

EXTRA SPECIAL - Dinner in a restaurant on the top of a mountain. Enjoyed a small train ride just to get there.

From the first day in Rome to the last day also in Rome and everything in between, a very special time in my life.

What a trip!!!!

WHAT A GIFT
- MY FRIEND

Angela and I met while working and connected. We are different in length of years, marital status, race, education, and skill level but we saw something in each other that made for a life time friendship. It goes like this.

One of the things that makes his friendship special is that, despite the Midwest bias, my singlehood is not a problem. Since she is not originally from KC, she doesn't see being single as a difficult or competency issue. Very good for me.

She was married and had three children who live in California, New York and, are you ready for this? Australia. And now, can you hear the drums and bugles? She is a Grandmother. I get pictures of the new member of her family. A good GrandMom.

Now, the big one at least in this day and age. We are racially different—she is African-American and I am Caucasian. As amazing as it might seem, while we both appreciate the differences, we do not see them as problems. We have frequent discussions regarding race and culture and view our respective comments and opinions as thoughtful and more often than not as a learning experience. Our friendship has given me new insights into the racist world that, sadly, is still here.

When we met, she had an undergraduate degree and I did not. I retired and got both undergraduate and graduate degrees. Angela subsequently told me that I was her "role model" and she was going forward to get her Masters. She did and got it from one of the most difficult MBA Programs in the country. I was definitely flattered.

I'm older and remind her periodically that because of this multi-year difference, I'm right about everything. Her response or responses are usually very funny.

She subsequently moved from the Midwest to North Carolina to be near her birth family. I was in full support of her decision since KC was not her home base but the east coast was. Both of us are busy in a variety of activities that reach into our respective communities.

We are in touch frequently and she is another one of my life's gifts.

THE SIBLINGS

No, not mine but to one another and all three were exceptional people. Before I left KC for San Francisco, I met, along with my family, most of this family such as a Mom, Aunt and five boys. Both girls were in other parts of the country and I got to meet and know the one noted below. I am so grateful that I got to know these three because each one had and still has a special spot in my heart and life. Here they are................

MARY: Actually, you have already read all about Mary earlier in this journey. Early on, she was my Decision Maker and that played a very vital and important segment in my life. As you will note, she was smart, practical and had a wonderful personal warmth. Because we visited in the late 1950s and the times were somewhat restricted for women, her life and conversation put her way ahead of her times.

FRANCIS: If you only met him for a few minutes, you would always remember him. He was one of those people in this life who were so special. He was my gift.

We both were retired and had moved back to the Midwest which gave us time to get to know each other a second time. It's hard to explain the effect he had on people who met him but here is a story that might help. He attended a party at my home along with my work colleagues and friends and relatives. A great party, lots of fun and I imagine that most of my friends from work probably chatted with Francis for five or ten minutes. Months later when we lost Francis and I was away from work to attend the funeral, my colleagues wanted to know who had passed away. I started to tell them that it was a retired priest and good friend who…………….and in each case before I could finish, someone would say "Francis?" or "Was it Francis?" and other questions but always with his name. After a very short visit many months before, they knew who I was talking about and they were saddened. He simply had that effect on people.

During his last illness, I went to see him and told the hospital staff that I was his cousin so I could get into the ICU. When I told him I had just become his cousin, he said "tell them you're my sister, you are." We had a one hour talk that I will never forget since he left this life a few days later. I still reflect on my good fortune being the friend (sister) of Francis.

And………………………………

MICHAEL: The baby of seven and a great addition. He became another brother for me. Not unlike his brother and some members of my family, he became a priest. His initial assignment was as a Campus Minister at a couple of universities in the Midwest, and then he spent thirty plus years as a missionary in South America. A very good and caring priest.

When we both wound up in the Midwest once again, we connected many times but especially in these two:

First, we got together for dinner and conversation and much laughter and our similar interests and views on life made for interesting visits.

Second, and from my own personal view, I liked to pick on him and reminded him, since he was my "brother," that I was always right about everything. As you can appreciate, he responded appropriately.

Great friends, wonderful siblings, and my time with each was exceptional.

CLOSE CALL - THE THIRD

In the early 2000s, I was flying from Albuquerque back to the Midwest. During the take-off roll, the plane blew a tire and some rubber was sucked into one of the engines. The engine imploded versus exploded which was fortunate but because the plane was too far into the take-off roll, we were airborne with one engine and one landing gear.

While the commercial airport and adjacent Air Force Base prepared for a crash landing, all of us on the plane spent the next two hours facing our mortality. A very reflective and soul-searching time.

Since we had what I believe to be the world's best pilot, he was able to keep the plane's wings level and we landed safely at the Air Force Base.

And, 139 passengers plus crew gave a collective sigh of relief, joy and thanksgiving.

As my Grandmother would say to all,
"Your work is not done yet."

FUN STUFF

Shortly before I retired, I had to have my gall bladder removed. I told my colleagues at work and friends away from work that I would give them a gall stone after surgery.

Before the surgery I purchased a bag of small but beautiful marbles and while at home during recovery I prepared these gifts.

Each marble was wrapped in tissue with a bow and an enclosed note that said the following:

"Some of us just have better looking gall stones."

I then put each stone in a padded envelope and shipped them off to about a dozen or more friends here at home and around the country.

Great fun. All recipients were appropriately grateful.

MORE BUSINESS

LEADERSHIP STYLES: WOMEN AND MEN, DIFFERENT?

Absolutely, women and men lead differently. I've worked long enough to have had excellent and not-so-excellent female and male leaders/managers/supervisors. In my view, the differences are only occasionally associated with basic intelligence or work product knowledge. It is usually a matter of style over substance. There are peripheral issues connected to the style of leading i.e. tone of voice, body language, hand mannerisms, emotional disposition, connectedness to people, people management skills, etc., but the major differences frequently fall at the feet of prejudice. Consider the following:

First, many of the prejudices associated with a female leader are attached to the perception that she lacks male supervisory or leader attributes. I respectfully suggest that this concept runs both ways in that many male leaders could use a few inherently female work traits.

Second, we must deal with lifetime experiences or biases on the part of followers. These predispositions tend to form a thought pattern aptly identified in the following quote from the Talmud that says; "We do not see things as they are but rather as we are." In other words, adjusting to change is a difficult task.

Finally, and perhaps most important, there is a belief on the part of some men and women that the male leadership standard is the standard for all. Big mistake, very encumbering.

Bottom Line: Women and men are obviously very different—physiologically, anatomically, brain patterns, how they dress, think, conceptualize, verbalize, drive, multitask, love, hate, and on and on. So, my question is:

HOW COULD THEY NOT LEAD DIFFERENTLY?

SEASON SIX

RETIREMENT
AND
SCHOOL

HANGING OUT, NO ALARMS,

OLDER STUDENT, MORE LIFE

PLANNING, WHAT FUN.

PRE-RETIREMENT PLANNING

WHEN: Shortly after starting first job.

WHY: Akin to planning for a trip—-I need to know where, how, directions, cost and, above all else, what to do when I get there.

I worked a very long time and retired somewhat late in life but all to a good purpose. I enjoyed what I was doing, the money was good, and that combination set me up for a more relaxed and mostly free from worry retirement. Was I rich? No, but comfortable which means that I had enough discretionary funds to take care of problems should they arise. Here's was my plan.

First, I set an approximate retirement date and since I knew I would retire late, I started my planning somewhat late too. Then I did all the financial planning looking at the present and future so I would have an idea of my finances or lack thereof twelve years or so down the line.

Second, I took a really good look at where I wanted to live. For instance, staying in the Midwest, or back to the West Coast, or elsewhere and then, as much as possible, looked at probable expenses at all locations. I loved the West Coast so that was my first thought but, frankly, when looking at both locations, I would not be able to afford my first choice. Midwest it was!

Third, I needed to decide whether I wanted to continue renting or own a home. I decided on the latter and purchased my first home which was one of my smartest financial decisions.

Fourth, made a list of the material things and/or equipment I wanted to own without debt. I had a list of around twenty items, from new car to home equipment to special equipment to allow me to hear music, and I noted the expense of all of it.

Fifth. Was I going to travel? Yes, but mostly within the U.S. to see what I had not seen before and spend time with my friends who had become family. I established a reasonable travel fund.

Now I was ready. It was in the 2000s and time to go. **CARRY ON**......................................

RETIREMENT
- FINALLY

After many, many years, four major urban areas, too many temp and permanent positions, I'm finally stepping off that ledge , backing up to age 16 where I wasn't making money. YIKES!!!!

Now I had my frequently up-dated financial and material planning accomplished. What was left was the emotional side of leaving something I had been doing for most of my life. A big decision but made easier by being what I've been my entire life which is a good planner.

Was I uncomfortable or worried about this big step? Yes and no but I relied on my planning and was comforted by the good friends at work who would still be good friends.

The entire HR Staff had a going away and good luck party at my supervisor's home. Lots of fun with colleagues, spouses, and other family members and there was great support and encouragement as I moved to another phase in my life.

I am pleased that I am still in touch with some of my colleagues. We do lunches, dinners, etc. and a very nice connection continues.

Final question regarding retirement is as follows:

I asked myself what had I always wanted to do but couldn't because of working? Easy answer — SCHOOL!

BACK TO SCHOOL

A LIFETIME DREAM
COME TRUE

Retired on a Wednesday, entered the University on Monday. No time to waste.

During the past ten years that I worked, I would now and then take a night class at a local college or university. Much to my surprise, I had completed two years, therefore, I started my class room return as a Junior. For a learning junkie, it was the best.

I entered a smaller university with a main campus in Kansas and a smaller campus in the Kansas City area. The school had agreed to a reasonable accommodation due to my hearing loss. We jointly decided that my instructor would wear a transmitter with a small microphone and I would wear a receiver with an ear bud and this would allow me to hear no matter where the instructor was standing or facing. It was further agreed that I would not take a final exam but would submit whatever written paper was requested. I was home, happy and learning. Great school.

I entered an accelerated adult program that compressed the 16 week semester into 8 weeks. It was intense and my accommodation to write a paper in place of a final exam along with the normal written assignments during the 8 weeks provided much attention to the written word. It could not have been better.

I enjoyed two and a half years (with a semester off now and then) of satisfying my low boredom threshold. Classes were interesting, writing was fun, and I was learning all the time. Loved every minute.

I received my BA, Magna Cum Laude, with a major in Psychology and Human Behavior and a minor in Women's Studies. What an exciting time. Finishing college was tying up one of life's loose ends. Two of my family members hosted a reception in my honor the day after graduation. What great fun to see and visit with friends and some family. Something about graduating from college when one is this long in the tooth got everyone all fired up.

Shortly before graduation, one of my professors suggested that I consider going forward and seek a Master's degree. I explained that this had not been on my "life's list" but would give it some consideration. After much thought and discussion with friends and my professors, I decided to move forward with another degree. Just before starting my MA program, the school offered me a part time position getting everything ready for a state review of the school. I worked 10 hours a week and this paid for the entire first year of the MA program. Once again, I was very fortunate.

An example of how intense an accelerated Masters program can be is demonstrated by my class in Managing a Culturally Diverse Workforce. During this 8 weeks of learning I wrote 15 papers. It was fun, interesting and somewhat tiring. I was all "written out" when I finished.

I received my MA in Human Resources (with a 4.0 GPA) and, once again, what a moment in time it remains for me.

TAKE NOTE: There is something very special and different and fun when one is older than her professors.

Speaking of those professors, a special nod to all but especially to............................

Sybil: She was the first professor I contacted when I was looking for a university to accommodate my hearing loss. She assured me they (the university) would do it. They did. Then, I was fortunate enough to be in a few of her classes—-what a wonderful learning experience. We are still in touch.

Peter: He was my instructor during my first undergraduate class and he went out of his way to be sure that I could hear everything. During one class, he rearranged his teaching schedule to give me time to go home and get my hearing receiver which I had forgotten. I was willing to go without it, he wasn't.

Karen: Another great learning experience and interesting classes. She encouraged, advised, and stepped forward on my behalf when there was a problem regarding the hearing issue. A great instructor who offered suggestions on my written word and made sure that all her students knew the subject. Everyone learned. What a woman.

Tom: Great teacher and advisor. He taught my last class in the MA Program and he always made sure that we knew the subject. Because I wrote so many papers in the eight weeks, he read and commented on everyone. As I was finishing my senior year in my undergraduate program and was starting my planning for my MA, his advice on classes/subjects was excellent. I was fortunate to have him advising me.

INTRODUCTION TO.......................

SCHOOL PAPERS

SO, in every mention of going back to school and the accommodations for my hearing loss, I mentioned writing, how much I enjoyed it, that it was my strong suit, etc., so I decided to give you three examples of papers written for a class or classes. Here they are:

MEN JUDGING MEN - This from my Master's Research Class and as you can see, there was considerable research. It is not meant to annoy or offend but rather to be interesting and thought provoking.

LAW AND CONSCIENCE w/ADDENDUM - Frankly, I'm not sure what class but it was a somewhat up to date subject following digesting Plato's dialogue, The Crito, and Sophocle's play, Antigone where we were presented with polar opposite views of our responsibility to the law. I found it interesting to write on this current subject but as noted, very sad for all. The Addendum brings it up to date.

HEARING LOSS—A PERSONAL CONNECTION - This was unusual in that I wrote it at one sitting straight out of my gut. No research or discussion, rather when I saw a picture of that painting, I simply sat down and fired away. When I was through and read it, I was stunned.

Hope you find them interesting.

ENJOY!!!!!

MEN JUDGING MEN

This research is dedicated to the hypothesis that men do a poor job when evaluating or judging the actions of other men. It will briefly look at this phenomenon from a number of perspectives i.e. law enforcement behaviors and gender issues, but most important, will be the cultural aspect which includes a significant sports mentality with a primary attachment to the male sports arena.

First, and for the sake of clarity, it is possible that male (or female) law enforcement officers might have some problems judging other men, but it is more likely that their training and experience will move them in the direction of making their decisions based on facts rather than gender. While one of the non-judgment examples involves some law enforcement officers neglecting to administer a breathalyzer test, this situation was more motivated by a strong sports mentality connection.

Second, this hypothesis is truly not a gender issue, i.e. males versus females, since the evidence and experience is heavily weighted on the side of the male population. Having said that and based on the sports mentality causes, women may be catching up with males in that they may find it difficult to sit in judgment on other females. At the current time, however, the female involvement in sports is still lagging behind the fully involved male participation, so the judgment factor for women is not yet completely evidenced.

Finally, after researching all the possibilities, this phenomenon is determined to be a cultural matter, born in the sports arena that begins with grade school, high school, college, and professional sports, and then carries that judgment mind-set into the non-sports social and business world. We will set the foundation of this research by reporting on the following examples and then take a look at possible causes.

The Big Three of Non-Judgment

We start with the most publicized and most egregious incidences of the failures of men to judge men. There is a similarity of cause and patterns of behavior in each of these three cases that deliver a frightening lapse of responsibility on the part of the males accountable for a moral code in a well-populated environment. These cases are Penn State, the Boy Scouts of America, and the Roman Catholic Church.

PENN STATE: As early as 1998, school officials received reports of inappropriate behavior on the part of Jerry Sandusky (Nitney Lions Defensive Coordinator) directed toward ten and eleven year old boys. These reports triggered an investigation that was subsequently closed at the request of the head of the campus police. In 1999 Sandusky retired from the football program but retained his access to campus facilities including the locker room. In 2000, a janitor advised another janitor and his supervisor that he saw Sandusky engaged in sexual activity with a boy in the assistant coaches' shower. The supervisor's response was to advise the janitor that he could report the incident if he chose to do so. In 2002, Mike McQueary, a graduate assistant, reported to Joe Paterno, the football coach, that he saw Sandusky sexually assaulting a boy in the showers. On the following day, Paterno passed this information on to Tim Curley, the athletic director, and in a subsequent meeting with Curley and Gary Schultz, the school's Senior Vice President, McQueary reported the same information that he gave to Paterno. No report was made to police or to any child protection agency.

Still in 2002, the school took away Sandusky's keys to the locker room and he was banned from bringing children onto the Penn State campus. These decisions were approved by Graham Spanier, the university president. Once again, there was still no report to the proper authorities.

Finally, in 2009, the mother of a boy called her son's high school to report that he had been sexually abused by Sandusky. The police were notified and in 2010, McQueary testified to the grand jury that he reported this behavior in 2002 to Paterno, Schultz and Curley.

Eventually, all of the players except McQueary lost their jobs with several charged with making false statements to the grand jury or failing to report the possible abuse of a child. All of these men, starting with McQueary, followed by a senior vice-president, the coach, the university president, two janitors and their supervisor, and the Penn State general counsel were aware of the reports and accusations resulting from Sandusky's behavior and not one of them reported it to the proper authorities (Chappell, 2012).

BOY SCOUTS OF AMERICA (BSA): Covering the time period of 1965 to 1985, the BSA maintained approximately 1,200 "perversion files" each naming an alleged child molester banned from Scouting by the Boy Scouts. They fought for decades to keep the files secret but finally lost a legal battle in Portland, Oregon, and the files were made public and went online in the fall of 2012. These files contained an estimated 14,500 pages of material, including internal BSA memos, newspaper clippings, criminal court records, and BSA notifications to alleged perpetrators that their Scouting credentials were being revoked.

The same situation arose in Texas wherein a number of Scoutmasters and employees were reported to have engaged in pedophilia. Their offenses involved multiple victims and the molestation took place on campouts, at the victim's home, the Scoutmaster's home, in the back seats of cars, and in the buildings where the pack or troop gathered for meetings.

As with Penn State, although many BSA employees were made aware of these incidences of molestation, they were not reported to the proper authorities. The BSA hierarchy kept the files as noted above but did not take appropriate action (Parks, 2012.)

ROMAN CATHOLIC CHURCH (RCC): In the United States, the accusations were made public by way of a civil lawsuit filed against the Church by an alleged victim and this started in the mid to late 1980s. A flood of accusations followed through the 1990s and into the first several years of the new millennium and these covered a large number of the Catholic clergy. Starting in the early years of the 2000s, the dioceses in the United States adopted strict policies and processes in reporting this abuse the result of which is that most accusations in the past five or six years refer to alleged violations going back forty to sixty years.

Two issues were more evident to the RCC and both have severely complicated the legal issues and certainly damaged worldwide opinion of the Church. They are: 1) excessive media attention both at a national and international level wherein only accusations are front page news whereas recantations and proof of innocence are rarely covered by the media; and 2) the false accusations some going back over fifty years have complicated the legal problems and investigations.

The Church, as with Penn State and the BSA, received many reports of inappropriate behavior directed at school children and they failed to report these behaviors to law enforcement or child protection agencies.

There are two common denominators attached to the actions of the Big Three. First, all accusations were against men and were then received, reviewed and evaluated by men and over a period of many years, these men failed to make the required notifications to the appropriate authorities. Second, while the crimes involved cast a significant shadow on any entity, large or small, it was clear that in all three cases, efforts were primarily dedicated to protecting the good name, reputation and the male hierarchy of the University, its football team, the Boy Scouts, and the Catholic Church. Sadly, within that dedication, they failed to protect the children.

The Smaller Four of Silence

The following are somewhat less publicized incidences of a failure to judge. Two of these made it to the national media, one was more publicized locally, and one is a first person account of a disciplinary case in Los Angeles. Regardless, they are indicative of the same culture as dictated in the larger cases. These are as follows: Steubenville Rape; Rutgers University; Los Angeles Threat; and KCMO Police Department.

STEUBENVILLE RAPE: This rape occurred in Steubenville, Ohio, on August 11, 2012, when an incapacitated high school girl was publicly and repeatedly sexually violated by two high school football players. For approximately six hours, this girl was taken by the accused from party to party and photographed. While several other football players observed the rapes, no attempt was made to stop the violence and further, they did not report it to the proper authorities. The rapes and subsequent criminal charges only became public when some of the photographs were posted on the social media (Wikipedia, 2013.)

RUTGERS UNIVERSITY: The men's basketball coach, Mike Rice, was fired from the University on April 3, 2013, for verbally and physically abusing the players on his team. As early as September, 2012, the Athletic Director, Tim Pernetti, gave Rice a fine and suspension for this same abuse. Although Pernetti, an Assistant Coach, and the Senior Vice President and General Counsel of the University were aware Rice's abusive behavior, the decision to fire him came only after video clips were made public in the first few days of April, 2013. Along with Rice's firing, the assistant coach resigned on April

3, Pernetti resigned on April 5, and John Wolf, the General Counsel resigned on April 11. It is interesting to note that Rice and Pernetti both received buyout packages in excess of $1 million each (New Jersey Journal, 2013.)

LOS ANGELES THREAT: In a disciplinary case involving a reported threat made by a male employee toward a female employee in a federal facility, the Employee Relations Manager and two other middle managers, all males, were assigned to interview the alleged threatener. After the interview, the middle managers were instructed to report on the interview to the incoming case manager who was a female. In their verbal report, both managers indicated that the accused was not a problem because "we could have taken care of him". Upon questioning, they said they could have physically restrained him. They were advised that their role was to risk assess the accused and they again said they could have taken care of him. Within the next 48 hours both managers returned, separately to the incoming manager and reported that they found the accused a "very scary guy" but they could not say this in front of each other (Weaver, 1989.)

KCMO POLICE DEPARTMENT: The KCPD observed a male asleep in the driver's seat of a car with the motor idling at 3 AM on Linwood Boulevard. They awakened the driver and discovered he was Jovan Belcher a popular and successful member of the Kansas City Chiefs' football team. The two police officers summoned two other officers and the four men had a discussion with Mr. Belcher. The police report said Belcher displayed possible signs of being under the influence but after a few minutes his demeanor and communication became more coherent. The police allowed Belcher to stay in an apartment located on the same block and the two women in that apartment invited him to wait in a nearby empty apartment. These two women said that Belcher "appeared to be intoxicated." A few hours later, Belcher shot and killed his girlfriend and then himself. Approximately seven hours after the Linwood

Boulevard KCPD/Belcher conversation, Belcher's blood alcohol level was .17, more than twice the legal limit to be sitting behind the wheel of a parked car with the engine running. The police officers were so content to have a conversation with a Chief's football player that they missed the obvious critical link in this event—no breathalyzer test was given to Mr. Belcher (Hollingsworth.2013.)

Silent Witness Causes

As we digest all of the examples where a failure to judge and/or report a breach of rules and regulations or a criminal offense, there are some glaring commonalities of cause. Taking this a step further, these lapses of judgment would seem to fall under the male sports culture umbrella. Specifically, this culture is being identified primarily as the masculinity syndrome (the perils of macho) which includes the sports/locker room mentality and the I ain't no snitch policy. As mentioned above, it is apparent that there is an emotional and cultural fit between the seven examples and all three causes.

MASCULINITY SYNDROME: Masculinity is a continuous process that must always be played out and a man cannot let his guard down for fear of revealing weakness. It follows then that taking a stand and judging another man as wrong might be seen as a failure. It begins early in life as a boy is evaluated for his masculinity by his father (or mother) and he must prove himself to his family and eventually his peers, bosses and other males (Goodloe, 2011.)

This masculinity culture is a never-ending test and is defined more by what one is rather than who one is. Playwright David Mamet has written that what men need is men's approval. A boy is evaluated his whole life, seeking approval from other men, fearful of what other men will think or being exposed as vulnerable (Goodloe, 2011.)

The consequences of this culture would seem to set males up to build a wall of silence when it comes to reporting a transgression on the part of another male or males. The merger of our examples and this cause would seem to support this cultural connection.

SPORTS/LOCKER ROOM MENTALITY: It starts in the locker room and then takes itself onto the playing field and beyond and it is deeply rooted in a multi-generational male concept (Diegel, 2012.)

Locker room mentality is rampant within the inner sanctum of male sports. It's a boys-will-be-boys mentality that is acceptable within that mentality, however, the gap between acceptable behavior behind this closed door and closed mind mentality, and acceptable behavior in any other workplace must be narrowed (Hayes, 2005.) As we've seen in the examples, it is simply unacceptable behavior when this mentality allows inappropriate and criminal behaviors to continue and flourish because of a culture that impedes doing the right thing.

I AIN'T NO SNITCH POLICY: Snitching on your teammate breaks a moral code in the locker room. The attitude seems to be "I'll take a cheater over a snitch any day of any week (Diaz, 2011.)" Once more we face a culture that is acceptable and expected in the sports locker rooms. As we carry that culture into the social and work worlds, we have men unable to judge men simply because it would break the code of silence. Teammates on a sports team and colleagues at your place of work are the same since you are on a team, hence, snitching whether in the real locker room or the analogous locker room in an office, presents the same issues for men. In every single example offered, we see the No Snitch Policy in action.

Yogi Berra has offered the following: "You stand up for your teammates. Your loyalty is to them. You protect them through good and bad, because they'd do the same for you." (Berra, 1989.) Protecting through good and bad says it all—Yogi spells out the culture.

CONCLUSION: After researching and reading no less than twenty-five articles on the subject of judging, men judging men, women in sports, men in sports, and snitching, I was astonished at the information that was available on the examples given regarding men judging men. I thought I knew the complete story behind these examples. Clearly, I did not. The only one, of course, that came as no surprise was the Los Angeles Threat since I was a part of that investigation.

There is no doubt that men have a difficult time judging other men and the causes seem reasonably reliable. The sports and locker room culture for boys, young men, middle-aged men, and older men, remains the same and it all comes down to their masculinity. Deep inside the heart and soul of any man, there is a vulnerability button that no one wants pushed or made public. He will protect it in a number of ways not the least of which is letting all within range understand that he is "the man." With that self-concept and because most men recognize the same vulnerability in each other, it makes it very difficult if not impossible to "rat out" another man. They simply cannot do it. It has no serious malice aforethought, rather it is an autopilot reaction born and bred in their own personal sports culture.

The consequences of this culture are evident in all seven examples. It defies good judgment, casts a pall on integrity, and halts any semblance of moral responsibility. The decision makers in all of these incidences knee-jerked themselves into protecting the wrong parties—their culture didn't allow for an honest and appropriate judgment of other men.

We need to eliminate the idea of judging other men and replace it with the concept of calling it (the situation) like it is. What if we advise all the men in the Big 3 and Small 4 to not judge but rather just report out the situation in a very honest and accurate manner regardless of the gender of the participants. Clearly, our society of men needs to understand the males judging males dynamic and start the process of evaluating any and all situations with integrity and then making appropriate reports as necessary. Applying that idea to our seven examples gives one pause to consider the agony that would have been avoided, the institutions that would have survived with their reputations intact, the lives that might have been saved, and the children who would have been protected.

In the spirit of sports mentality, I call on the men of the world to step up to the plate. The time is now.

References

Berra, Y. (1989). Thoughts and Quotes.

Chappell, B. (2012). Penn State Abuse Scandal: A Guide and Timeline.

Diaz, G. (2011). Who do you despise more? A cheater or a snitch.

Diegel, A. (2012). NFL's 'Tough Guy' Culture Does More Harm Than Good In Long Run.

Goodloe, A. (2011). Masculinity in America: Men Judging Men.

Hayes, N. (2005). Locker-Room Culture Is Unacceptable.

Hollingsworth, H. (2013). Jovan Belcher Autopsy: Chiefs LB Legally Drunk At Time Of Murder-Suicide.

New Jersey Journal, (2013). Rutgers basketball scandal: The key people who took the fall.

Parks, S. (2012). Online release of Boy Scouts' 'perversion files' breaks decades pf secrecy.

Weaver, B. (1989). Confidential Threat File. Unpublished Report.

Wikipedia, (2013). Steubenville High School rape case.

LAW AND CONSCIENCE
(w/Addendum)

I have watched with interest the continuing battle over one of the most divisive issues in this country, that being abortion. It is a law versus conscience issue that will, in my view, never be completely settled. I've been involved in this issue peripherally and find it a sad and difficult situation with everyone, on either side of the conflict, firmly believing that their side is right. There is no room for compromise.

When having an abortion became legal and wound its way through the legal system to the Supreme Court, the Court did not rule on the efficacy of abortion but rather on the constitutional right of a woman to make her own choice. That was an appropriate decision given that the underlying question of when life begins was not put before the Court.

A woman's right to make her own choice is doing battle with the various Christian groups who believe in their heart and soul that there is life at conception, hence abortion constitutes murder. The Christian groups cite as their argument their religious beliefs and that there is a heart beat as soon as 20 days after conception and that heart beat is life. The pro-choice groups believe that if the fetus cannot exist outside of the womb, there is no life; however, this argument has been somewhat complicated by the approval of late term abortions where the aborted fetus could live outside of the womb.

So, we have a classic law versus conscience issue. The law that supports a woman's right to choose whether or not her fetus will go to full term, and a conscience that believes that abortion is murder since there was life at the moment of conception.

Now to the big question—when does life begin? Unless or until a credible non-religious, scientific body can say precisely when life begins, there will be no answer to this question and sadly the conflict will continue.

ADDENDUM

TO

LAW AND CONSCIENCE

This school paper was written considerably before the recent Supreme Court reversal of the 1973 Roe V. Wade decision. The recent Supreme Court decision dated June 24, 2022, declares that the constitutional right to abortion no longer exists.

Upon review of this LAW AND CONSCIENCE school paper and considerable discussions with my editors, we have decided that the law and conscience issues themselves have not changed and are still with us even with the Supreme Court's change in constitutional thinking.

With or without Roe V. Wade, the law and conscience concept regarding abortion will remain in the hearts and souls of most women and many U.S. citizens.

Red Hills with White Shell
By
Georgia O'Keeffe

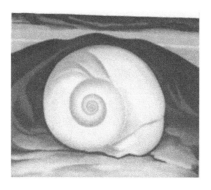

TOUCHED BY ART

BRYN WEAVER - A PERSONAL CONNECTION

If I only allow myself a visual look at this painting, I determine that it is a white shell covered by a red mass since I did not see the hills, and the shell is imposing in its size and clarity but seems stuck and surrounded by that red mass.

My visceral impression was immediate and made me stop and study. I saw a portrait of my deafness and as I studied this painting, I experienced the same sadness that my lack of hearing imposes on me. This is not a white shell—it is a magnification of my cochlea completely devoid of sound conductors. What is interesting is that even in that overblown and magnified state, the microscopic hairs that capture sound are gone. I thought I might see the hairs if only in a state of falling down, but they are simply missing. What is left is what Simon and Garfunkel called The Sounds of Silence.

The red mass above the cochlea is a shallow mass of tissue

and bones including the tympana or ear drum that is designed to protect those conductors. It is ironic that this mass now protects an empty cochlea and it sadly reminds me of the noise of the past and the muffled sounds of the here and now.

Above the red mass, there is a band of yellow that is narrow in the middle and somewhat broader on the right and left. This has become my electronic corridor since it houses the wires that lead to my cochlea and stimulate the auditory nerve in my brain. It is part of the hearing miracle—my implanted bionic sound conductor.

The very top red and gray edge of this painting of my sound loss is my emotional roller coaster and while it looks a little flat, I can see within the colors, the up and down movement. The up-side constitutes my daily gratitude and relief as I experience the joyful results of the surgical miracle that allows me to electronically hear a portion of my life. As my roller coaster car moved down I come face to face with my limitations in restaurants, stores, listening to music, attending the theater, and being able to enjoy normal or real sounds. Or possibly, I am simply confronting my grief.

FUN STUFF

From my captioned phone. Two characteristics one must have in order to successfully manage such a phone. First, a lot of patience, and second, a great sense of humor.

During a phone call with a friend who does some work for me, she mentioned that "my Father had some falls." My machine printed that he "had some balls." Given that her Dad is very elderly, I started to laugh and shared this caption with her. She started to laugh and we finally hung up since we were out of control with laughter.

A few hours later she called me so we could finish our business. She then shared with me the following:

"I told my Dad what your caption phone said about him and he asked me to tell you that he's very pleased."

What a guy!!

SEASON SEVEN

NEW PATH

ALL THAT

HARD WORK,

PLANNING,

SCHOOL,

VOLUNTEERISM,

CRITICAL THINKING,

GOOD FRIENDS,

PRAYER,

FINISHING HOMEWORK,

AND

CHOCOLATE,

PAID OFF.

NEW PATH

Awesome task! Now I must take all the experiences and joy and relationships and learning and make it all work in a good, happy, charitable and productive way. I never saw myself sitting at home, watching TV, cooking (yikes), and doing very little. Lets face it, I'm a people person and like to be active and above all else have always felt I have an obligation to assist and take care of others in one way or another.

The original plan after I finished my Master's was to teach but as time went on, my hearing loss became more difficult. My loss was considered post linguistic which meant that while I had full speech and could hear the sound of a voice, I frequently could not distinguish the words. With the cochlear implant, eyeball to eyeball conversations were easy but in a class room with possibly more than one voice at a time, or a voice not being directed to me, much would be lost. Hence, no teaching.

So now, what to do?? Three ideas came to mind based on experience, education, skill and, what I consider, doing for others. HERE WE GO..........................

First, if I've learned nothing else, my time in the "trenches" of the hearing impaired world has qualified me to work in this area, so I've been giving power point presentations to a variety of groups. My approach is to the practical, not medical, side of this impairment. For instance, after one gets hearing aids, voices frequently sound different; or teaching the people in your life how to deal with an audio loss whether their own or someone close; or how to deal with the emotional side of this impairment. Also, one of the more interesting parts of my presentation is dispelling the myths surrounding hearing loss and this segment is frequently fun.

These presentations are given to a variety of groups such as senior's meetings, school instructors and students, church groups, some federal agencies, small customer related businesses and occasionally big business. Most of these programs are given on a no charge basis with the exception of big business—-they get a statement of charges.

In addition to this program, I've been assisting the elderly poor in getting grants for hearing aids. Very simply I do the considerable paper work connected with these applications. Think about it, who better than a retired "fed" to do your paper work? Got it?

Second, due to twenty-five years working in human resources, I consult with two specific groups. Mostly, I've worked with and consulted with people, young and older, looking for a job. My assistance is along the lines of writing resumes, interview skills, and question and answer practice that might come up at an interview.

The other group is usually the small business owners/managers who need some assistance in the hiring and firing areas. One gentleman I worked with was frequently belligerent which was a surprise since I was there at his invitation. He advised/discussed how he manages a small, mostly female, staff and then he asked in a very annoyed tone, "Just what is it you think you could do for me?" My response after listening to how he treats his employees was, "keep you out of court." After a long sigh and deep breath he said, "good thought."

Third, I do some consulting and referrals with friends and relatives who may have experienced emotional problems at home or in their careers. I don't do long term counseling but my years in education and experience in the world of psychology have given me the knowledge to know how to calm a situation and offer suggestions not the least of which is making referrals where necessary.

The only other area in which I'm involved is miscellaneous

volunteer efforts through a variety of facilities. This is always interesting and good for the people I help and myself.

Is all of this fun? Yes. My planning paid off financially and the part-time tasks are interesting and gratifying.

AND all of this book takes us back to my early belief that not-so-good beginnings and some physical issues should not spoil the entire journey of life. Maybe my policy is to continue to MOVE ALONG. Once again, thank you for being here.

AND in the words of St. Francis de Sales, BE AT PEACE.

FUN STUFF

For years I have exercised daily by walking on the treadmill and doing some strength training. My length of walk is between a mile and a half and two miles. I credit this consistency with my moderately active life style.

During a particular walk, I slipped and started to fall forward. I was saved by moving my leg forward and catching myself. I was rescued from what might have been a dangerous fall but that leg effort caused a pulled hamstring muscle. As I'm sure we all know, since the hamstring muscle goes directly down one's backside, I had a very sore tush.

I stayed at home for several days, since standing and sitting were a problem so decided to have some fun and include others. It went like this: I sent an email to around a dozen friends that read as follows:

"For all of you, who all these years, thought I was a pain in the ass, it has finally happened."

What fun to do!! The best response, was a two word email that said the following: "About time."

It still makes me laugh.

SEASON EIGHT

DESSERT
AND
ALL THOSE EXTRAS

OPINION

IT'S NOT ABOUT ME

The United States Congress is charged to support and defend the Constitution of the United States and then be responsible to their employer who happens to be the people who voted for them and put them in office. Perhaps some Senators and Representatives actually take this seriously and work for us but not many. For the most part each party opposes anything the other party favors. It's about big business, big money, lobbyists, paybacks, earmarks, favors, and heaven help us all, politics. It is not about me.

Does either side of Congress offer their views, with specifics, so I can weigh both sides of an issue and make an informed decision? No, because they don't care about me or what I think. They only use the term "American People" when it suits any particular argument. What we have is a put-down culture that does not offer another direction or try to effect compromise but rather says that whatever is on the table won't work. So, I'm stuck with two groups whose wins and losses are not measured in terms of the people but rather which political party got the most points. Like I said, it is not about me.

Think about it, being noisy, finding fault with everything, offering no viable solutions, engaging in name calling, adopting a "my way or the highway" position, and getting more press is not the answer. It still won't be about me.

Consider for the moment the fact that we the people pay

congressional salaries in excess of 94 million dollars per year. This includes Senators, Representatives, Majority/Minority Leaders and Speaker of the House and it does not include all of the perks attached to these positions. My humanity is not part of the congressional equation, therefore, I'm suggesting to Congress that they go back to their roots and remember who they work for, who pays their salary, and who put them in office.

Ladies and Gentlemen of Congress of all stripes, colors and parties, I respectfully call to your attention the fact that the entire process in which you are involved should be all about me.

Sadly, it is not.

TWO CONGRESSIONAL THOUGHTS

1. If one would like to slow down the aging process, run it through Congress.

2. If the voyage of Columbus had been left up to Congress, his ship would still be at the dock.

OPINION

THE TIME IS NOW

Everyone in this country be they black, white, or any other color or ethnicity is sick of the killing. We can't take it anymore. The events of the past and present are simply beyond our ability to comprehend and rationally absorb. Not one person or group be it a matter of racial color or ethnicity or occupation or gender, can now afford to sit back and point the finger of guilt at another group. It has become an equal opportunity tragedy. We are all the worse for it.

Look at the senseless loss of life in Columbine, Sandy Hook, Orlando, Dallas, San Bernardino, Ferguson, Baton Rouge, St. Paul, Charleston, Las Vegas, Sutherland, Atlanta, Boulder, Indianapolis and now Buffalo, Uvalde and Tulsa, and then reflect that over 400 lives have been lost needlessly. We are all enraged, gut wrenchingly sad and emotionally exhausted. It is time to stop this deathly train of loss.

A fitting close to this opinion is from Tony Blair, the former Prime Minister of Great Britain. He said the following:

> "Understand the causes of senseless killing and racism. Yes, we should try. But let there be no moral ambiguity about this. Nothing can ever justify the killings and massacres and ambushes of the past and present and it is to turn justice on its head to pretend it could."

THE TIME IS NOW.

GREAT PEOPLE

FAMILY CONNECTIONS

As you read about my family, please bear in mind that I marched to a different drummer as I grew and, therefore, did not follow my "role" in this group. Was I difficult or in trouble or obstreperous? No, just frequently or occasionally, depending on the situation, I followed a different path.

When considering parents, I can say they were appropriate providers but as noted in my life's paths, it is obvious that the emotional connection was lacking as I was growing up. I remained connected to them all their lives because it was the right thing to do, even when I relocated to the West Coast.

My Grandparents were a mixture but my maternal Grandmother was sensational. She had wise and sometimes funny comments and was supportive of me all my life. My Great Aunt who lived with my Grandmother had remained single but was successful in her career—she was also one of my favorites.

I have two brothers and my connection to each one is very different which should come as no surprise when considering that most of our family connections were to say the least, complicated. My relationship to one is a kind of a "yes, no, maybe" situation. We have periods of good communication and times of no connection or relationship, but overall, I will always continue to communicate and be there when needed.

My most positive and loving family member is my older brother. He has and does stick with me through thick and thin. Given our home situation, I was so fortunate to have this guy in my life. We were in grade school and high school at the same time although he was a couple of years ahead of me and, even with that small amount of life's time separating us, we still connected. That connection never changed even though our adult lives moved us to different geographical parts of the country and our individual life's path moved in different directions. One trait that we both enjoyed in each other was our respective sense of humor. Between his wit and my tendency to see life's funny side, the relationship was always there and solid.

As we got older we took several trips together and since we were fond of big cities, we hit New York City, San Diego, Chicago, and San Francisco and wherever we were, our shared common interests got us to the theater, concerts, shopping, and art galleries. Two really exceptional trips deserve mention: first, to Houston for my first World Series game; and second, he invited me to take part in a group tour of Italy and, of course, another big city—-Rome. This was a once in a lifetime adventure. Great friend and travel companion.

Have I been sad that the entire biological family was not close? No. Despite the emotional complications, I've been able to keep the fond memories. I started making peace with this situation a long time ago and then had the added positive of my friends who filled in the gap with love.

Not to worry, however, the three siblings continue to have good lives with all three dedicated to charity and taking care of others.

AROUND THE COUNTRY

* Jane and David - Jane and I met when she was 18 and I was 24. She was in San Francisco going to school. The friendship grew from there to visits with her and her biological family in Southern California and more good times in San Francisco. She married David, who became one of my favorites. This wonderful relationship lasted through their three children, my frequent stays at their home in SoCal and a life long family connection. My relationship to their boys has also been long term. They are Richard, Greg and Mike and here they are.

Rich - Still in touch. We connected to become good friends. I call on him for a variety of ideas.

Greg - The middle guy who would skate in front of his house for hours waiting for me to show up.

Mike - The baby and when he was 5 and I was 31, we were engaged to be married. I cancelled that since he wouldn't leave kindergarten and get a job before we were married. To this day he still refers to me as his "former fiancée."

The entire family moved around the country and so did I but the love and connection never wavered. Once again, I am fortunate.

* Sandy and Ron - What a great couple. Ron and I were friends in San Francisco in the guest house. He met Sandy, they married and continued to live in SF. They are great fun, witty, smart and very generous—-their home is my home when I'm in San Fran. We continue to connect after all these years. Great friends.

* Pat and Bob - Pat and I worked together in the Pacific Northwest and at one time, she was my immediate supervisor. She was unique, very bright, one of a kind and marched to a different drummer. Since I marched to that same drummer, we have been life long friends. She became and remains a very special person in my life. Her youngest child became a good friend so let me introduce you to....................

* Kristi - She was a teenager when we first met and was one wonderful and very goofy teen. I have framed and hung on my wall some of her more hilarious communiques. She brought out the silly and goofy in me. Then she became this wonderful grownup who exhibits great charity towards others. I flew across country to attend her wedding and our friendship remains to this day. She and her husband have two children who are both in college and she does some teaching so I frequently ask what she does with her spare time. We remain close and connect via phone and email and my visits to the Northwest. Another great close friend.

* JAZAM - Otherwise known as Jason and Amanda and their three children with initials Z. and A. and M. hence JAZAM. During my Human Resources days, one of my programs was the Student Program. Jason applied and came to get information from me, I found an opening for him, and a life time friendship was started. He got his BS and eventually worked and studied his way into law enforcement. Along came Z. and A. and M. and the entire family moved all around the country, from coast to coast, and four cities. Jas is connected to his job and family and Amanda is one exceptional woman who manages all five people and five moves. I've visited with them for several days and what a great time. Very fun and smart people with whom I'm very happy to be connected.

* Marla - We worked together in KC and that connection jumped over her relocation to Colorado and my retirement.

The friendship has continued through the many years and she is just one terrific and very smart friend. Her position in Colorado took her to higher places so much so that she is in charge of people, programs, and ideas for a very large entity. Fortunately, we see each other at least once a year when I'm visiting friends and relatives in the Rockies and we frequently connect during those years via email and phone. Great person, wonderful friend and owns a marvelous sense of humor.

* Joyce - Another work colleague who also moved to another part of the country. However, it didn't deter our friendship. Her time away from the Midwest and on the East Coast was fruitful—she got a better job, returned to school and got a Master's Degree. During all this we were in touch visiting, communicating via email and phone, and continuing a wonderful relationship. We sometimes discuss problems which is a blessing for both of us. How grateful I am to have a good listener with a gentle heart and smart advice.

AROUND THE CORNER,
MIDWESTERN

* Carol is close. We grew up together having been next door neighbors until we were in our late teens. While our lives moved in different directions and locations, we remained in touch and connected. In many ways, we were very different i.e. religious affiliations and home culture, but our care and love for one another persisted. During my first vacation travel on my own, I visited with her in New Jersey and I have a picture of both of us, two nineteen year olds, at the Jersey Shore. What a memory! She has been in my life since I was eight years old—we go way, way back and up to the moment—for which I am grateful.

* Kristen is exceptional. A Mom of three, has the top educational degree, and is in charge of a big program at a local university. With all this, to my good fortune, she has become a friend. Due to the pandemic, we get together to have coffee and/or tea, sitting on chairs, at a very large table, in the middle of my driveway—weather permitting. She was my "Boss" and a good one, during my part time working at the university. So consider, with all of this, she is a classy and considerate good friend. I think awesome is the word.

* Margaret is a cousin who is great fun. Physically she has a little more to deal with due to COPD but forges ahead and stays active. I admire her tenacity and courage. In addition,

she was another one of my editors and, even though I called her a nitpicker, she was invaluable. I came to realize that a little nitpicking is beneficial. She has children and grandchildren and siblings all of whom are cousins. We visit frequently and I'm happy that we are in touch and connected.

* Emilee is amazing. Think about this—-she grew up in a small, conservative, Midwestern town where the opportunities were limited. Along with that, an early marriage failed and still nothing stops her. She continued to move upward. She got her undergraduate degree, then her Master's, and then moved back to the Midwest where she obtained her Ph.D. and she is currently teaching at one of the Midwestern universities. Looking at all that, she is my friend and a very gifted one. She is the role model for the phrase "Nevertheless She Persisted".

* Bobbi is unique, one of a kind, has lots of kids and grand-kids, and is very smart and was one of my editors. She lived at one of the senior independent living facilities and I started attending church services there on Sundays and fortunately got to know her. So, on Sunday afternoon, for four or five years, I would spend a few hours in her apartment visiting. After her children were grown, she went back to school and got her BA—-an adventure I could relate to. We still visit, and what is really nice, we can disagree on many topics with no backlash. A good friend.

CLOSING BELL

OK READERS, THIS IS IT!!

When I started this writing adventure, I told my friends, who are also my editors, that if I did not get published it was alright. Frankly, connecting with all those memories and people, then transferring it from thoughtful and sometimes fun reflection to the written word was a wonderful experience. I've enjoyed every minute on the keyboard and in front of the screen.

Having said that, I hope you too have enjoyed reading about this journey.

Don't misunderstand, "Closing Bell" does not mean a permanent exit, it only means closing this part of the journey as written. As long as possible, the journey will continue with thoughtfulness, kindness, helping others and continuing to view life's funny moments.

So, thank you again. Don't forget that every day is a gift, make it joyful, take care of yourself and others, have some chocolate, laugh, love, and especially remember that when it comes to kindness and goodness and generosity, The Time Is Now.

Bryn Weaver

ABOUT THE AUTHOR

The truth is that as a child and teenager I cultivated a soulful and experiential independence. It came from being aware that the adults in my life were unreliable, and without that independence felt I wouldn't have survived. I cared for people but in the end I depended on myself. That part of my early journey greatly contributed to who I am and who I became.

To this day, I continue in the same directions of caring for others, thoughtfulness, kindness and humor that I know to be my best way of moving forward. I remain in the same embrace of my many families whose vital practical support has been bestowed and lovingly received as a token of something much deeper.

The people in my life around the country and around the corner are often surprised, sometimes annoyingly so, that I am as content as I appear without someone.

My response to that is "not to worry". It has been a joyful and interesting journey with my many friends lovingly filling in that space in my life with friendship and love. I have been very fortunate.

Blessings to all and thank you for reading.
Bryn Weaver

MY EDITORS

AND THEIR COMMENTS

Angela - Fayetteville, NC - Reviewed entire book for continuity of subjects.

Comment: "Lots of time for so many subjects."

Bobbi - Kansas City, MO - Looked at writing from a business perspective.

Comment: "How come I get the boring job?"

Carey - Cheyenne, WY - How to get ready for publishing.

Comment: "Prepare patience."

Margaret - Kansas City, MO - Our nitpicker.

Comment: "No punctuation mark escapes my notice."

Excellent reviewers of my written word and great fun.

ABOUT ATMOSPHERE PRESS

Founded in 2015, Atmosphere Press was built on the principles of Honesty, Transparency, Professionalism, Kindness, and Making Your Book Awesome. As an ethical and author-friendly hybrid press, we stay true to that founding mission today.

If you're a reader, enter our giveaway for a free book here:

SCAN TO ENTER
BOOK GIVEAWAY

If you're a writer, submit your manuscript for consideration here:

SCAN TO SUBMIT
MANUSCRIPT

And always feel free to visit Atmosphere Press and our authors online at atmospherepress.com. See you there soon!

.